Klaus Hartwig Stoll

POINT ALPHA

Hot Spot of History

Michael Imhof Verlag

Klaus Hartwig Stoll: POINT ALPHA • Hot Spot of History
Michael Imhof Verlag, Petersberg 2007

© 2007   Michael Imhof Verlag GmbH & Co. KG, Stettiner Straße 25, D-36100 Petersberg
          phone 0661/9628286; fax 0661/63686

Design and Copy: Michael Imhof Verlag
Print: Fuldaer Verlagsanstalt, Fulda
Printed in EU

ISBN 978-3-86568-239-0

Table of Contents

Foreword

For many years it was considered to be one of the hottest spots in the Cold War – the former US observation camp "Point Alpha". Here at the interface between liberty and bondage, in the center of Germany and the legendary "Fulda Gap", armed to the teeth and always ready and able for the extreme, the two large power and military blocks of the world stood face to face: NATO and Warsaw Pact. This was where, one believed then, in the worst case and with high probability even a Third World War would find its start. When, with the peaceful revolution of 1989 in the GDR, the Wall and Border fell, Point Alpha had lost its function; it had done its duty. The authorities planned for "the Renaturation". Citizens of the region rebelled against this iniquity against history in the middle of the 1990s. The US Camp could be saved; it was placed under monument protection, just as the opposite border check systems, towers and ground bunkers of the GDR Border Guards. In 2003 the "House on the Border", which dedicates itself exclusively to the perfidious border regime of the GDR, was added to the Thuringia side. Both components, the former US Camp and the "House on the Border", together with the preserved original and the faithfully reconstructed border check systems, comprise today, on about 75,000 square meters, the memorial place Point Alpha – a singular memorial and an authentic testimony of recent German history, a real "learning place of history", as once a large German newspaper called it. Point Alpha reminds today of 40 years of sorrowful separation of Germany; it is against forgetting, playing down and falsifying, and most certainly against the occasional demands to draw the line on the still much too feeble attempts of an offensive and comprehensive "processing" of this terrible part of our history – as far as history can ever be processed. Nothing may be forgotten, not one of the violating acts of this inexpressible SED regime may be surpressed! If for no other reason than for the sake of the innumerable victims. Too much is still unknown, also unpunished, and still awaits compensation, if that is at all possible. Too many terrible things occurred in this time, to simply sweep them under the carpet of history. Everything possible must be done, and then more, so that such inhuman dictatorships are never again able to gain control. Peace and liberty – that is the message of Point Alpha. Hundreds of thousands have visited the memorial place since its opening in 1995, and the numbers increase year for year. This is reassuring and encourages the sponsoring association Border Museum Rhoen "Point Alpha" (registered association) to continue insistently on its chosen path. This book also wants to make a contribution. I thank very cordially also the equally insightful as knowledgeable author Klaus Hartwig Stoll and everyone involved in this band, particularly the numerous time-witnesses from Hesse, Thuringia, and the USA for their reports and the friendly provision of photos and other important documents.

Berthold Dücker
Chairman of the board

An Area of Disquiet – 1945–1952

Border Trespassers, Smugglers, Fugitives

When the German Army capitulated in May of 1945 and the weapons finally fell silent after five years of war, nobody expected that the quiet place, where the pine bend their tops towards Geisa to the valley of the Ulster, would one day be considered to be the hottest spot of the Cold War. This area and the current Warning, Memorial, and Meeting place "Point Alpha" mirrored for nearly half a century the history of the post war era. The

top: Barrier on the B84

bottom: Street barrier in the early 1950s

moss covered, rarely noticed border stones in the vicinity turned into much more important symbols over the years. Up to now, they had separated the two previous German States – Prussia and Thuringia. Their engravings marked, as of 1945, the demarcation line between the Russian and American occupation zones. This turned into the border between two German partial states in 1949; the Federal Republic of Germany and the GDR. From now on, this line separated the Western and the Eastern world. Two political systems, one of freedom and one a dictatorship, were separated by this line. Two military power blocks stood face to face. In addition, should a battle occur, this was where the attack was expected to take place. This was where the armies confronted each other; this was most likely where the first decisive battle would take place, using the most modern destruction weapons. Thank God it never came to that.

In July 1945, when the Americans, following contract, pulled out of Thuringia and the soldiers of the Red Army advanced to the border of their occupation zone, things became hectic and dangerous. Only a few hundred meters from Point Alpha was Fischerhof, a solitary farm in Thuringia, as was common to the Rhoen. Not even twenty meters away were the border stones. They had been set in 1815 as the Geisa district of the Prince Bishopric Fulda fell to Sachsen-Weimar, whereas the Western part of the clerical Principality fell to Hesse and later to the Kingdom of Prussia. KP and SW were therefore engraved on the stones. From Fischerhof only a few steps were needed and one was in another zone. This was a goal which many strove towards. Many people were underway in both directions. Families which had been torn apart during the war wanted to reunite and avoided the formalities of the regular crossing. Village residents visited their relatives in Thuringia and vice a versa. Others preferred to get out of the Russian Zone until it was too late; the Russians plundered their zone systematically to get the promised remuneration of 10 million dollars. And, as at all borders, smugglers carried out their business: American cigarettes for Russian alcohol. Who ever was caught by the patrols of occupation troops had to spend a few days at Katzenstein near Andenhausen or had to go the Hünfeld Ratskeller. Therefore there were reoccurring arrests. At one escape attempt even the death of a young girl in the area of the farm was reported.

Fischerhof was not the only good place to cross the border unnoticed. The somewhat thirty mile road from Wenigentaft to Spahl was well populated. The villages on this side and on the other were in good sight of each other with only a few kilometers between them. The landscape was open, there were no high mountains to hold up the refugees, and small forests offered cover. The locals knew their way around in the area; they had spent years using the short cuts to visit their relatives in the neighbouring village or to go shopping in Geisa – the economical centre. This all favored the crossings. In every village, there were adventurous young people who were prepared to help the refugees and bring them to the border – a dangerous life.

In summer of 1946, the zone borders were closed. Turnpikes on the streets offered only a symbolic barrier: on the field paths and the side streets entire households and even businesses could transport their belongings to the West. The farmers were stilled allowed to go back and forth to cultivate their fields. A special pass allowed them to cross. But, as the currency reform in the West filled the shelves, more important things came up. In Rasdorf, everything which couldn't be bought in Geisa, was available;

top: Historical border stone at the Hessian-Thuringian Border (KP= Kingdom of Prussia)
The coat of arms shows with the double shield shows the initials of the Royal Family von Mansbach and Geyso zu Mansbach

Family Bednarek after the escape in May 1952

Fischerhof; the Border ran left in front of the spruce trees.

tools, household goods, shoes, spices for butchering and much more. But, how could one get West money? Every now and then, in agreement with a good acquaintance, a cow would be driven across the green border to the West and sold there. With this money the Thuringian could go shopping in Hesse. Eggs, poultry, and of course alcohol were envied articles also in the West. Hamster trips out of the interior of the Russian Zone were worth it if one could find a secret path and a place to spend the night.

The controls from the occupation powers were sketchy. Russia and America occupied a number of areas on the border after 1945, where the patrols took up their path on foot or by jeep. The Russian huts along the street from Rasdorf to Setzelbach just outside Wiesenfeld were feared. US troops laid in tents in Setzelbach and Rasdorf or just outside of Buttlar in the so called

"Ami-Forest". Barracks were set up in Geismar and Geisa for the Russian troops. From there the observation points were occupied. The complex in the Geismar district is partly still intact as well as the ground bunkers of the Red Army on the mountain Rockenstuhl. The grounds there were temporarily barred to the citizens because the view into Rasdorf Mountain was possible from here – the area where the Americans had begun to set up camp. The Americans soon understood that the border patrol could not be carried out from their garrison in Fulda. The march was too far. They set up observation points from which the border crossing could be seen. There were also ground bunkers which were supported by beams and covered with a tarp. It was possible that such posts on the grounds of the future Point Alpha might control the street from Rasdorf to Geisa. There is evidence of a post in the so

The Buchenmühle house, in front the border fence, probably in 1953

called "Ami-Forest"; a thicket south of the crossing at the B84. Another, on the mountain Hellenberg, controlled the Taft valley with the mill Buchenmühle. Further back, border camps were set up where the troops and vehicles were accommodated for a time. Later the observation point was extended. After 1946, West and East German police organizations took over the border patrols. Up to the sixties, it was the People's Police – VOPO – in the east. Beginning in 1949, the German Customs appeared in the West. But, with a bit of knowledge of the area, the border trespassers were able to elude them all.

After the end of the battles in 1945, most of the American troops were sent back to their homes and discharged. Remaining was one infantry division. Alongside this division, the so called Constabulary Unit was created out of varying troops. As its name reveals, this unit was to take over police respon-

sibilities in the interior and the control of the border. The 81st squadron of the 2nd regiment, which was stationed in Fulda, was equipped with an armored scout car M8, a 37-mm-canon and the light tank m24 (75caliber). The unit had to observe the district of Fulda and Hünfeld; the military division was, generally speaking, based on the current German districts. In contrast to the American Military Police – a German administration first came about in 1946 – the soldiers of the constabulary had a number of noticeable characteristics: yellow stripes on the helmet, the same on the vehicles, a large C on the helmet, and a yellow throat scarf among other things. They soon got the nick name Potato Bugs. They were not only feared by border trespassers, but also for their sudden black market raids in the cities.

Constabulary Patch

Complete view of Buchenmühle

Ten Meter Strip and Forced Evacuation – The 14th Armored Cavalry Regiment

In 1952, the adventurous activities came to an end. The tension between the USA and the Soviet Union had been developing since 1946. The communistic downfall in Poland, the Check Republic and in the Balkans revealed the aggressive character of the Soviet politics, which was also demonstrated in the Berlin blockade in Germany in 1948. The Cold War broke out. As a result, the West Zones combined and created and their own state – the Federal Republic of Germany. As answer to this, the German Democratic Republic (GDR) was created. At first, there was no noticeable difference at the border. However, it soon turned very serious. The GDR government decided on "actions for securing the border against saboteur, spies, terrorists and vermin". The police regulations from 27 May 1952 revealed the method which had been planned: a ten meter wide control strip, a 500 meter wide security strip and a 5 km wide barrier zone. The troops marched into Geisa from the interior in the first days of June. They fallowed the fields and the acres, and dug aisles in the forest in order to install control strips there as well. The citizens of the border area near the villages feared for their land which was on the other side.

But, this was not the worst. On June 5, a number of families in the city of Geisa, some 39, received the order to prepare themselves for "evacuation from the aggressive West powers" to the East on the next day. Furniture and utilities should be loaded onto carts. This news spread like fire from house to house. In no time at all the decision was made: outside we are removed, we will go to the West. A mass exodus began at the border. In Geisa, 24 of the affected families set out on their way. 150 persons from Geismar and Wiesenfeld arrived in the small village Setzelbach on this day, carrying only the absolute necessities, some of them driving their cattle with them. It was similar in Rasdorf and the other border areas from Mansbach to Tann. The general fear was that all border villages

Plowing the 10 meter strip on the inner-German border

would be evacuated. The action "Vermin", as the first wave of evacuations was named had begun. Out of the 353 citizens in the Bad Salzungen District, 113 families were affected. The goal wasn't at all to evacuate because of danger, but rather to intimidate the citizens and make them willing to be evacuated. The long arm of power selected the victims based on previous oppositional behavior, and contact to the West and – who didn't have contact in this area? Other victims had a Nazi history or were convicts. But, some were also innocent citizens. The local government had created a list which lay in the hands of the Mayor. The Eastern and Western administrations were completely surprised by the exodus. A unified system of orders was missing. Therefore, the refugees were sometimes able to go and get further items from their homes over the next days. Over a thousand people fled in the district of Hünfeld and Fulda.

In the following months the ten meter strip directly behind the demarcation line – the imaginary line from border stone to border stone – was dug up und leveled, and a meter high barbed wire fence was erected in front of it. The first barrier now stretched over mountains and valleys.

But how did it come about that after 7 years the border was suddenly completely closed? The GDR offices explained that these precautions served as security against the aggressive West; especially the Federal Republic of Germany (FRG). They had just closed a general contract with the West powers. This contract allowed FRG far reaching sovereignty, with the stipulation that they collaborate militarily in protecting West Europe, which was acutely necessary after the break out of the Korean War in 1950. They believed that the separated Germany could, as in the example of the separated Korea, also be attacked by the communistic constituent state. The West feared, as did the East, a war. The consequences of the Cold War became noticeable at the border zone.

However, the barrier precautions had another reason and this was surely more important. They should stop fugitive escape out of the GDR, which threatened to increase. In April 1952, the Soviet Union changed their strategy in German politics. Instead of plundering the

Soviet zones, as they had done up to then, they decided that Germany should now be turned into an industrial state. This meant a heavier work load for the citizens, which was demonstrated in the increased work norms for everyone. The control strip was not intended to deter the Western agents, but rather fugitives out of the East.

Becoming very clear with the Berlin blockade in 1948 and even more clearly with the Korean War in 1950, the conflict between the Soviet Union and the USA took on ever sharper forms. America saw themselves forced to maintain a larger troop force. The Constabulary Unit was reorganized and increased a number of times. Their responsibilities were redefined: instead of police assignment, which in the meantime had been taken over by German forces, they were now to deter a feared attack from the East. Three constabulary battle units were now in the American occupation zone and ready for action. Each was equipped with 51 tanks, 72 armored scout cars, 18 self-propelled howitzer, grenade launcher,

Armored crew wagon M113 A2 of the 14th ACR

tank destruction weapons and pioneer units. Furthermore, the 14th armored cavalry regiment (ACR) was set up at the end of 1948. The ACR took over Constabulary Unit bit by bit and incorporated it. In 1959, this was accomplished and the Constabulary Unit was officially disbanded. The 14th regiment stood in the full tradition of previous mounted troops of the USA. The motto which could be read on the sleeves of the soldiers was "suivez moi"– follow me. Their units wore the typical cavalry insignia "Squadron" for the battalion and "troop" for the company; the soldiers themselves were troopers. But the strategic tasks of the riders – reconnaissance and surprise intervention – were long since taken over by armored vehicles. The name cavalry remained however, since the regiment was a reconnaissance troop; the extra term "light" was used. The Fulda regiment was supposed to control the border from Herleshausen to Mellrichstadt; therefore the three squadrons were barracked outside of Fulda in Hersfeld and Kissingen.

Mood Swing: Easing of Tension and Escalation – 1953–1972

Continuous Disquiet on the Border

The fear that a third world war could break out, didn't turn into reality. After the death of Stalin in 1953, power struggles followed in Kremlin, which Chruschtschow finally managed to win. In the meantime the Soviet Union had also developed the hydrogen bomb. As a result the power blocks saw themselves in a situation in which they could be both destroyed. This stale mate desperately demanded a phase of peaceful co-existence from the East and the West.

At the border it definitely looked different. The hoped for effect of the barriers did not take place and more and more citizens fled the "state of workers and farmers". The disappointment of the citizens about the politics exploded on 17th of June in 1953 in a national uprising against the planned increase in the work norms. The announced new course was able to pacify only for a while, and then 100,000 to 200,000 refugees arrived yearly in the West, most of them via West Berlin. Alone in Fulda, the federal border control registered 60 to 70 refugees monthly.

The responsibility of controlling the border remained in the hands of the Americans and the Russians only in the first years after the end

Soldiers at the 10 meter strip. The photo was brought by a refugee in 1956

Officers of the Federal Border Security (BGS) on duty

of the war. Afterwards German units also participated in the controls. The Hessian Border Police was to control cross border trade. In Tann and Hünfeld commissionerships were set up. With the founding of the FRG all of the responsibilities went the Customs Control. The Customs Officers as they were called by the citizens, were under the Finance Ministry. The troops were armed only with pistols or carbines, but they always had a dog with them. As long as the smuggling bloomed, their main duty was to deter the import of illegal commodities. After the closing of the barrier in 1952, their task changed to the observation of the opposition and the aiding of refugees. After the break out of the Korean War, the Federal Border Security (BGS), a police troop which was under the Ministry of the Interior, was formed in keeping with the Cold War. It had infantry weapons, but was also armed with the American armored M8 scout car and a special armored crew car. They were supposed to be able to stand up to the Soviet Zone barracked People's Police, which was being established, and prevent border trespassing. The nearest locations were in Fulda in 1952; as of 1959 there were more in Hünfeld.

Border fence in the 50s

On the East side, alongside the Russians, the East German People's Police (Vopos), in their blue uniforms, had also taken over control duty. As the Vopos were accommodated in private homes, a good relationship to the citizens and the West German Customs officers held for some time. In the fifties the units in the border villages were quartered in huts, later in barracks. In the beginning of the sixties the border troops of the Nation People's Army (NVA) took up their duty, with the special task of deterring escape out of the Republic. In the West they were called "Grenzer" or "Gresos" – custom officials – and wore gray uniforms, which looked similar to those of the German Military. The opposing regiment had their staff in Dermbach, with more companies of the responsible 2nd Battalion in Geisa, Geismar, Wiesenfeld and Spahl.

After the installation of the 10 meter strip, more and more incidents occurred at the border. In 1953, Border Security was called in for the first time. The mill Buchenmühle, located about 4 kilometers from Point Alpha, was positioned in the solitary valley of the Taft. The

demarcation line ran directly down the middle of this property. On the West German side was the mill, the old house and the barn. On the other side a larger, newer house and the well. During the installation of the 10 meter strip an entrance to the property was left open. Otherwise, the border was secured with barbed wire and poles. As the Russians also closed off this entrance a bit later, the owner of Buchenmühle called the Border Security for help. In a lightning action, a unit arrived early mornings, opened the barrier, and cleared out the house and the tool shed completely. A guard was positioned for some time in the barn to deter attacks.

In September 1956, the public was occupied with the mysterious death of a GDR border policeman, Waldemar Estel, at the crossing on the B84 just outside Buttlar. A Mercedes with two Spaniards drove up to the turnpike. The strangers made contact with two Vopos, who had been working on the 10 meter strip. One of the policemen went with one of the Spaniards down the street towards Buttlar – avoiding the turnpike by going over the field was absolutely no problem. The other policeman gave two signal shots to call for reinforcement. As they could be seen coming around the corner, the Spaniard attacked his companion, drew a pistol and fired directly at Estel, who, hit fatally, collapsed. The Spaniard fled to the car, was shot at by two policemen, but he was not hit and was able to escape unharmed with his companion. Border Security, Customs and criminal investigators from West and East met at the turnpike to investigate the case together. The motive for the murder was never clarified.

In 1960 a serious incident took place in Setzelbach, where the bor-

der was only a few meters behind the last houses. A group of Vopos appeared, stretched a long rope between two border stones and tried to gain a piece of land for the East, which up to that time had been excluded from control strips, by removing turf and digging a new control strip with a small bulldozer. The outraged citizens alarmed Customs and BGS. The Vopos didn't react at all to the protest of the Customs officers. Only after the Border Security arrived out of the manned area of Hünfeld – which had been established in 1959 – did they begin to negotiate. It became evident that the Vopos had been

Uniforms of the People's Police and the Reserve Police

using an old map. But, they departed only after the BGS officer ultimately set a deadline and set up his riflemen in position. A guard was also placed here for a number of days for security.

The atmosphere at the border turned threatening. Some trespassers were met by the waiting Vopos with aimed weapons and arrested. The contact to Customs officers broke. On Good Friday 1961, just outside of Seiferts in the high Rhoen, a few young men, who had camped on the boulders of the Bildsteins just a few meters from the demarcation line, were chased away without warning by a raid of machine gun fire. One of them was seriously injured through a lung shot. Only through use of a US helicopters, was it was possible to medically treat the injured man in the Fulda hospital. The marksman in the year 1961, whose name was known by the trespasser, was accused and convicted – admittedly on probation – after the reunification in 1999; 38 years later.

The increasing numbers of visitors headed to the border zone in the West brought new responsibilities to the border control. After the 17 June was proclaimed day of the Germany Unity, although not only for this date, even more visitors streamed – even in buses – to the remarkable border points; to Buchenmühle and, above all to the streets of Rasdorf-Setzelbach, which ran directly along the border. All of these were in the area of Point Alpha. Already in 1954, this place, Point Alpha, from where a

BGS (Federal Border Security) and US soldiers discussing a control run.

view far into Thuringia was offered, had been determined as a place for a commemoration ceremony in 1954. On the previous evening, a wood pile was set afire and the victims of 1953 were commemorated. The annual ceremony, organized by the curatorial an Inseparable Germany, brought in important politicians. In 1964 a large event took place on the meadow in Rasdorf. The, at that time, refugees from Geisa and surroundings had united in a homeland circle which met each other every few years in the area of Point Alpha; a location where one could look down on to the area. Later they erected a memorial stone to commemorate those places of the "Geisa District" which had once belonged to Fulda. In the spring 1960, when the Gov-

Street barrier on the Federal Highway B84

Setting of concrete posts for the double fence

ernment of the GDR had forcible installed the complete collectivization of agriculture and the farmers were pushed in the "agricultural production cooperative" (LPG), serious difficulties in supply arose. The stream of refugees swelled again. The Government decided on radical action; the building of the Wall straight through Berlin, on 13 June 1961. Everyone could now see that the GDR citizens had become "disfranchised" and were living in a prison.

That substantial changes in the border would also take place became clear already in the same year. One could observe that several families, in the so-called "action Cornflower" – the second wave of forced evacuation – were once again forcibly removed. Farmsteads

Demolition of the abandoned house of the Buchenmühle in the year 1961

in the border vicinity were also demolished, for example the "Auszugshaus" of Buchenmühle, only a few kilometers away from Point Alpha. Fischerhof had already been razed. Further areas that were hit in the closer vicinity: the Wassermann- and Jakobshof near Spahl, three farms in Reinhards, the Schlehmühle between Ketten and Apfelbach, the Seleshof near Walkes and the entire Langwinden hamlet just outside Motzlar, as well as several farmyards further south.

Double fence and Fire Exchange

The next year brought the most dangerous incident at the border in the area of Point Alpha, and it caused a death. In summer 1962 pioneers of the national People's Army (NVA) moved forward and began erecting a new fence in the area of Rasdorf-Setzelbach, which was guarded by its comrades. A few meters behind the demarcation line, they rammed heavy, two meters high, concrete piles into the earth. They were connected by 12 barbed wire lines. In 10 to 20 meters spacing, a second such fence arose. One could have worked their way through with pliers, but mines had been laid in the gap between the double fences. An escape had now become an incalculable and deadly adventure. Some soldiers used their duty so close to the border as a final chance for escape. In order to hinder this, guards, whose machine guns could sweep the demarcation line, had entrenched themselves. BGS posts were activated on Western side to give the refugees cover. The situation was extremely tense. In Rasdorf and Setzelbach the work had begun. A platoon leader of the Wiesenfeld Company managed to

escape unnoticed. The tension increased. Would they soon open fire? The Border Control was permanently present, and the Americans had reinforced their jeep controls. On 9 August, after lunch, one of the artillery transporters was bringing the heavy concrete posts to the work site just outside of Setzelbach. But instead of stopping to unload, the track vehicle continued on its way direction west, drove down the barrier, rattled further into a tree orchard ripping off a tree limb, and finally stopped several meters on the Western side. Everyone was stunned: the village inhabitants who had been watching, the BGS officials and the American patrol, who had coincidentally stopped in the area. No shots fell, not even from the NVA guards. A soldier jumped out of the car, and threw himself on the ground. He had reached his goal, he was in the West. Immediate reinforcement arrived from the Americans and the Border Control, US helicopters flew overhead, and officers appeared. The tractor was quickly removed to a safe distance. An NVA officer demanded the immediate return of the soldier, which was naturally refused. For several days, the place remained occupied in order to hinder retaliation. The vehicle however received active attention from the Americans; it was transported into the USA, tested there and first exchanged after one year for an Army truck.

Only five days later, on 14 August, the feared fire exchange became reality, resulting in one death. Just outside Wiesenfeld, the border ran close along the road to Rasdorf-Setzelbach. Guards and Border Security lay face to face in position. It had to be avoided that Western visitors provoked the GDR soldiers. As a Border Security officer was mak-

The wooden tower on the OP Alpha which was erected in 1968.

ing his control run with two companions close to demarcation line, an NVA officer called out and ordered them to stop, because they were in Eastern territory. At the same time he delivered a warning shot. Since the officer did not react, the NVA officer aimed at the West Germans. The companion fired his machine gun. The NVA officer jerked and collapsed. Everyone involved dove under cover. A number of shots were wildly fired in all directions, but no-one else was hit. Then it turned quiet. A flare gun signaled the retreat of the work troops; the officer was removed. The report of his death was broadcasted in the news. There was no collective investigation of the incident. The East claimed a BGS officer had been in GDR area and had shot first; the West declared, the companion fired in justified self-defense. The deceased, Captain Rudi

NVA- Officers investigate in the afternoon of 14 August the grounds where the fire exchange took place.

Captain Rudi Arnstadt

Arnstadt, was Chief of the Wiesenfeld Company. He was from now on honored as a hero. The West German marksman, who later lived in Hünfeld and worked as a taxi driver, was found shot to death in his taxi between Hünfeld and Rasdorf after the reunion in 1997.

The rumors that this was an act of revenge, found no end. The case was never solved. The motive for the attack on the BGS officer became clear through defectors. Captain Arnstadt probably wanted to surprise and capture the officer, just like in previous frequent successes with occasional border trespassers. The officer should serve as an exchange object for the artillery transporter. The frequently honored officer probably felt such pressure from the escape of his platoon leader and the loss of the tractor that he reacted spontaneously.

US armed forces were not allowed to involve themselves in incidents at the border; their involvement would have increased the danger of war. They had to keep their activities to demonstrating their presence and observation duty. They had already intensified their observation of the enemy's intents. Part of this was ra-

Construction of the double fence

The old brickyard near Wenigentaft with the double fence

21

dio monitoring. In the mid sixties, the decision must have been made to extend Point Alpha and make it one of the four surveillance spots of the 14. Field commands. The decisive factor was that the radio traffic could be monitored best from here. Previously the "Ami-forest" with the view over Buttlar had been designated, but after thorough measurements, it became clear that radio monitoring was substantially better at Point Alpha. In 1965, the area was formally turned over to armed forces. It was surrounded by a fence; trees had to be cut down in order to store the armored vehicles which were stationed here. A wooden surveillance tower was built at the end of the decade directly on the demarcation line. And, in replacement of the tents, wooden barracks were constructed for accommodation. There were also re-

ports of a corrugated sheet barrack on the site of today's barrack C.

With the construction of the double fence, which dragged on into the next year, the refugee numbers suddenly decreased. Only a few refugees came over. One of them, through his attempt at Wiesenfeld, had to pay with the amputation of his leg after he had stepped on a land mine. It became quiet at the border. The double row of the bright concrete piles shone far into the distance; grass and bushes around them had disappeared. Only individual gates permitted entrance into the apron area, which was kept free of vegetation. Watch towers, at first made of wood, then of concrete rings soon arose in the countryside, trip wires and dog on running chains should additionally prevent any escape. The inhabitants of the GDR had to resign themselves

to the given conditions and make do.

A phase of relaxing also began in the political world. Chruschtschow had heated the situation in 1958 with his demand that Berlin should be a "Free State" and all occupation powers should retreat. The tension increased when he attempted to station rockets in Cuba in 1962, which threatened the USA. After the determined resistance of the USA, he retreated. Furthermore, the Western powers did not militarily react to the unlawful building of the Wall in Berlin – the effect of the atomic stale mate. Starting from the mid-sixties, the USA were increasingly busy with the Vietnam War. The Soviet Union however, did not dare to use this weakness to its own advantage in Europe. The two great powers had lost the German states out of sight. 14th Cavalry Regiment still performed its control duties at the border during this time and trained its forces for an emergency; in case the East attacked. It remained quiet in the area around Point Alpha up into seventies.

Closer contact between the Americans and the German population was allowed soon after the removal of the Occupation statute in 1952. In this sequence, numerous meetings on official and private levels occurred. In 1952, the Federal Republic received, by general contract and with only a few minor exceptions, full sovereignty. Finally, when the FRG became a member of NATO in 1955 and were able set up their own military forces, the American troops, once an occupation power, had now become allies who of course, with their exclusive possession of nuclear weapons, were able to unsure security in West Germany.

The double fence west of the Buchenmühle, the slope has been freed of undergrowth, below is the border line.

The Blackhorse Regiment Secures "Fulda Gap" – 1972–1989

Blackhorse Troopers in Point Alpha

Command Tower of the GDR Border troops between Rasdorf and Setzelbach

The world was in an unusual situation in the seventies. While the USA broke off their useless battles in Vietnam and withdrew their troops, a phase of easing tensions began in Europe. The Western powers and the Soviet Union met in 1971 for a

Power Treaty determining the status of Berlin, which had, up to now, always been contentious. The Federal Government took up negotiations with the GDR Government in the "Basis-of-Relations Treaty". In 1972, it led to a de-facto-recognition of the GDR, and in the "Traffic Contract", they brought some relief in the German-German traffic; they did not however achieve the opening of the border from East to West. In the same year, the USA and the Soviet Union agreed on the limitation of the nuclear weapons in the Salt Treaty, and in 1975 an agreement was reached in Helsinki, which offered „Safety and co-operation in Europe" as a future prospect (CSCE). All this pointed towards a lasting ease in the tensions. But only a misleading and superficial ease prevailed; the military of both World powers remained sceptical towards the peace efforts. Despite the atomic stale mate they counted on the outbreak of hostilities and made their preparations. The Soviet Union developed its strategy of a surprise and strong tank raid in Central Europe. In the USA, one expected this attack and prepared for it.

By no means, should the Russians get the impression that the Americans had resigned. Nearly as proof of their determined intent to defend Europe, the 11th Armored Cavalry Regiment – steeped in tradition and elite, successful in Vietnam – was stationed in Fulda in May 1972. It replaced and took over the 14th Armored Cavalry Regiment with its officer corps and a

Pioneers repairing the metal lattice fence. The guards are standing with their backs to the viewer.

A self-shooting mechanism is installed on the metal lattice fence

On Freedom's Frontier

11th ARMORED CAVALRY REGIMENT
FULDA, WEST GERMANY
First Edition 20. December 1989

Coat of arms of the 11th ACR

US soldier during the guard duty on the Observation Tower of Point Alpha

View out of the tower onto the border

part of its crew. The renowned fighting troop should guard the front most line of defense in the middle of Germany. The 11th Armored Reconnaissance Regiment wears a coat of arms with a jumping horse, therefore the name "Blackhorse". Its motto was „Allons!" – "Let's go!". The regiment received a double task; the continuous control of the border and the defense of deployment spaces in case of an attack from the East.

The first task was the surveillance and security of the border, and this task was closely connected with the observation Point Alpha. In addition, it was of greater importance

Special equipment on observation tower

US jeeps on patrol

Mine sweeping vehicle of the GDR Border Troops

for the soldiers than training the emergency case, which nobody wished for. Here, with the duty at the border, everyone could see that they were defending liberty. Only too noticeably recognized, was that on the other side behind the barriers, a system prevailed, which had to stop its citizens by force from turning their backs on it. That was also easy for the simple trooper to understand. The service far from the homeland gained special meaning for the trooper.

He could watch how in 1972 the barriers were reconstructed. The mines were blown up, the double fence torn down and set back several meters and a three meter high metal lattice fence erected. Since this was carried out under sharp observation and with special equipment, there was no possibility of escape. Finally the notorious self shooting devices played down as harmless were mounted on the fences – splitter mines (SM 70).

Pioneers searching for mines at the metal lattice fence

Through touching a wire, they hurled sharp-edged metal slivers. The event, which took place directly under the observation tower before the eyes of the American soldiers, was oppressive. Late on 24 December 1975, in the dark, two fugitives detonated one of the self shooting devices. The guard sergeants could watch how a lifeless body was removed. It was said that he had been fatally injured. His companion was arrested. On the anniversary of this event, the Young

Union (youth organization of the political party CDU) of Rasdorf erected outside the North East corner a simple Birch cross as memorial. Several years after the reunion, the, at that time fatally injured, person appeared; despite heavy injuries he had survived.

Each company of the Blackhorse regiment could expect to be transferred for three to four weeks to one of the observation bases four times a year. Now it was important to observe the other military side and to listen to their radio contacts; controls were sent out to patrol the border and a number of troops were held ready for immediate action in order to man the tanks and army trucks in a matter of minutes. These troops, through the demonstration of their presence and their weapons, could also expect to be confronted directly with the oppositional border troops, whose weapons were loaded and aimed directly at them; these threats were reciprocal. Simi-

The Birch Cross in front of the Observation Tower

The fighter tank M1 A1 "Abrams" of the 11th ACR was equipped with a 120mm board canon.

lar activities were carried out by air. Helicopters flew in dangerous maneuvers close along the demarcation line and were able to see far into the opposite side. For many soldiers, the parting from family

Training consultation at the tail of the battle vehicle M577 A2

Battle break /battle tank M1 A1 of the 11th ACR during the training "Caravan Guard" in September 1989 near Westerburg

and spare time in Fulda was probably counterbalanced by these challenges.

The service for those approximately 30 soldiers began at six o'clock a.m. with a review of the preceding events at the border. After breakfast, orders were given with a thorough inspection of uniform, weapons and equipment. The troop should appear in an exemplary state, also for an unexpected visit. The troop itself, fitting to the orders, was divided in three groups.

Newcomers, petty officers and officers were assigned to the operational reserve. They wore their uniforms day and night, had to be ready for combat within 10 minutes, with weapons loaded, and

Radio wagon M1037 with two-wheeld trailer

The hallway of Barrack A on Point Alpha

Return from foot patrol

two armored crew cars. The group was used for the demonstration of combat readiness, whether at the border or for visitors and inspections. It could be reinforced by reconnaissance scout cars, two tanks and a group of garnet launchers. All of these vehicles were stationed at Point Alpha.

Another group of soldiers was intended for observation duty. Four men occupied the tower for 24 hours with surveillance equipment, binoculars, ground based radar equipment, warmth sensor equipment, and radio and monitoring equipment. With this equipment, a tank could be located even from a 10 km distance. After one and a half hourly surveillance the crew was relieved; duty however was 24 hours, around the clock.

The third group took over the patrol at the border. The patrol consisted of two jeeps each with a three man crew under command of a sergeant. A jeep was equipped with a machine gun; the other one carried the radio equipment. Every half hour a short signal had to be given from the exact point to which they were headed. If a signal was missing for over one hour, a helicopter was sent out to take up the search for the patrol. However, according to repots, such an incident never occurred. The controls could last up to eight hours, but were for the most part shorter. They were organized such that points were covered within 72 hours. Thereby the entire border within the Fulda area was patrolled every three days. The soldiers of these patrols came into contact not only with the German Customs officers and those of the BGS, but also with the border troops of the GDR. During these controls, the various work on the barrier could be watched, changes determined and troop movements in the countryside registered.

Radar equipment on the observation tower of Point Alpha with view on Geisa

Sometimes the referred to threats were used here; weapons aimed at the opponent, loading of weapons, wild starting and sudden braking along the demarcation line. The interaction with Customs and BGS was comradely. With a coincidental meeting – the patrol times were set up so that no paths were patrolled at the same time – experiences, cigarettes and sweets were exchanged. A typical German appearance, which was appropriately admired, was the large shepherd dog, which the Customs Officer led with him on his single patrol. The patrols in the often rugged terrain formed a special attraction, so that they were more popular with the soldiers than the reserve and observation duty.

The regiment maintained four such "Observation Posts" (OP); at Herleshausen the highway crossing was monitored by the OP "India". The same function was taken over

by the OP "Romeo" in the area of Oberstuhl. Both were manned through Hersfeld. The age-old Frankfurt-Leipzig connection between Rasdorf and Buttlar was controlled by "Point Alpha". The squadron at Kissingen held the OP "Tennessee", near the crossing at Eußenhausen. Point Alpha was

Observation equipment of the OP Tennessee near Eußenhausen (Bavaria)

US radio man during a patrol tour

considered the most important one and was well-known as VIP-Point, on which prominent visitors, also high-ranking state guests, were received and where the explosive border situation was best described.

Therefore the expansion progressed in the seventies. For those approximately 30 soldiers, who lived there, two sturdy barracks (Barrack A and B) were constructed of pre-built parts which were set on concrete foundations. B served as accommodation, in A was the command as well as the medical rooms and the kitchen; in C was the cafeteria where leisure time was spent, if the barrack was not used as dormitory in cases of overflow. The wooden tower was replaced by a steel construction. A high fence encircled the unit. A water pipeline

and drains had to be installed; the electrical supply from Waldhof was redirected and re-laid in the ground. The base had gained significance. In 1978, Brown, the American Minister of Foreign Affairs from Fulda, paid a surprise visit by helicopter. There are also reports of other routine visits of various US Ministers. For some years it had become custom that the Mayor of Hünfeld and the Fulda District Administrator visited the soldiers at Christmas and demonstrated their gratefulness with small gifts. Also the Member of the Bundestag, Dr. Dregger, previously Mayor of Fulda, liked bringing his guests to this unit; a place which documented the splitting of Germany so impressively. His successor, Dr. Wolfgang Hamberger, likewise

The aerial photo shows the grounds of Point Alpha. Right under the trees were the tanks. In the background Geisa: the most westerly town of Thuringia

The former entrance to Point Alpha

maintained particularly intensive contact to the Americans, in particular to the observation post Point Alpha.

Securing the Fulda Gap

The second function which the Black Horse Regiment had to take over was more difficult. The strategists in the USA assumed that a Russian attack would be carried out from furthest advanced area of the Eastern sphere of influence, the "Thuringian Balcony" which jutted into the West. The objective would certainly have been the Rhine Main area around Mainz and Frankfurt, the narrowest area of the Federal Republic. The shortest way lead through a hallow area between the Rhoen and Vogelsberg, which were formed by the valleys of Fulda and Kinzig. This had already appeared in the strategic considerations "Fulda Gap" (hallow, gap near Fulda) in 1965. The attack was to be met in the form of the "frontal defense". The lines of defense should be built up as close as possible behind the border. To accommodate this, the Vth corps was located

in the area of Frankfurt with the 3rd Armored Division and the 8th Infantry Division ready for deployment. In order to give these troops the time and space needed for deployment, the 11th Regiment had to maintain lasting resistance in Alsfeld-Hersfeld-Fulda, shield the deployment and carry out inquiries on power and intents of the opponent. If the main forces approached, they would take up the regiment, which would then be re-formed as reserve behind the lines. In order to be able to carry out this difficult order, numerous maneuvers were held, in Grafenwöhr on the shooting range, and in the neighbouring Hohenfels for the terrain maneuvers. In the regiment's history, it is reported that within the implemented competitions between the individual units, the regiment frequently earned an outstanding position.

It is noted that in 1977, in the USA, a strategy game with the name "Fulda Gap", which simulated the combat area, appeared in the stores. The players use the conventional as well as nuclear weapons. The controversial game is currently exhibited in the memorial Point Alpha.

At the end of the seventies the world situation had once again changed. A phase of general increase in armaments on both sides began. When the Soviets entered Afghanistan at the turn of the year 1979-80, the idea was strengthened that in Europe an attack could also occur. In the meantime, weapon technology had developed new rockets, which were more accurate than the cruise missiles and could be implemented from continent to continent over a distance of well over a thousand kilometers, and, equipped with smaller atomic heads, enabled a limited nuclear war without industrial centers being reciprocally extinguished. One feared that such a war in Europe could break out; whereby the USA and the Soviet Union would not be affected. The "SS 20" Russian rockets stationed in Poland were answered by NATO with the set up of the "Pershing" rocket and the

Airport Sickels with the coat of arms of the 11th ACR

"Cruise missiles" – remote controlled cruise missiles. The defensive measures were reinforced, which was demonstratively supported by the American President Reagan.

The Blackhorse regiment was primarily affected by this new strategy. As is the case of its predecessor, two squadrons were stationed in Hersfeld and Kissingen, while the staff and a third squadron were situated in Fulda. Their accommodations, "Downs Barracks", partially still originated from the times of the armed forces, and urgently needed to be enlarged and modernized; the regiment was permanently assigned new units and more modern weapons. The light weight Sheridan reconnaissance tanks were replaced by the heavier main battle tank (MBT) M 60 A3, then by the M1-Series ("Abrams"- 120 mm calibers). M 113 armored gunman wagon was dispatched from "Bradley". An artillery battalion with 24, 155-mm-

Helicopter base "Sickels Airfield" near Fulda aerial view

M60 in action

Haubitzen (M109 a2) was available, new ammunition cars for the front line, and even a new model jeep arrived ("Hummvee").

More important was that the helicopter fleet was renewed and reinforced. The "Blackhawk" was replaced by the UH-1D "Huey"; furthermore a modernized Scout Helicopter (OH 58 D) was used; in 1984 the "Apache" was replaced by the combat helicopter "Cobra". The helicopter base was the airfield in Sickels, which was from time to time filled with 74 machines, the largest helicopter fleet in Germany. It formed a 4th Squadron. Additionally, the regiment was attached to the "Combat Support Squadron", which was a versatile repair, supply and support unit with 366 soldiers. This 5th Squadron bore the name "Packhorse". The 58th Pioneer Company, a message unit and a ground based radar force completed the regiment. The total force amounted to 600 men, 530 track vehicles and 1,600 wheeled vehicles. The regiment with its modern and versatile equipment was a sought after mission area for ambitious officers. Two of the former commanders, Abrams and the

Franc, were promoted in the meantime to four-star generals.

The relation between the regiment and the German population was excellent, better than in some other Hessian garrisons. Whereas rather factual topics were discussed during the German-American and the Noise and Environmental Committee meetings, the contact club provided gatherings for the soldiers with Germans of the same age. More intensive relations developed through the approximately twelve cooperative sponsorships of the individual units with German towns or villages. For example, Hünfeld was associated with the Pioneer Company, Burghaun with the Delta, and Rasdorf with the Alpha Company. The Pioneers moved forward with their heavy crawler dozers, when it was necessary, to create a sports field. On this basis, numerous meetings were organized; invitations to family Christmas celebrations and invitations for coffee and cake or sausage and beer. Sports events, shooting competitions and fishing and riding outings amongst others, took place, depending upon the possibilities of the German municipality concerned. In Fulda, the German-American women's club still exists. The regiment sent out invitations to balls and to the regiment celebrations. On the other hand, the "Ami-in der Bütt", became a fixed component of the Fuldaer Carnival. The Christmas presents for the soldiers in the barracks had a long tradition. In the early period an „Ami- Nicolas" visited the school children in the villages close to the border. That these relations were carried by genuine friendship is proven not only through the pain often expressed when an officer was transferred from Fulda, but also through the fact that approximately 400 former soldiers of the regiment did not go back home after their discharge, but remained in the district Fulda.

With the increasing of tensions between the power blocks after 1980, Point Alpha became even more important in the case of a Soviet attack. With good reason it was defined as one of, if not the "Hottest Spots in the Cold War". A hanger for the vehicles and tanks was erected, the ground outside it paved with concrete and with a waste-oil dispensary supplied. Helicopters could now land there. A new tower, replacing the steel tower built three years previously, was built on concrete posts in 1985 in the northern corner of the area. Finally the entrance road from Geisaer Straße was paved as a tanker path. For many years it was controversial whether the opponent should see the arriving tanks or not; from the East, only the northern entrance road coming from

In place of the wooden tower, a steel tower was erected.

Felsenkeller could be seen. Now the decision for the under-cover entrance was made. After his entry to office, President Reagan ordered that each soldier, who did service in Germany, should convince himself of the oppression beyond the Iron Curtain by paying a visit to border. Subsequently, 20,000 visitors, who were brought in busses, had to be guided and informed. Afterwards, they were provided for at the Rasdorf village cafe Budenz. Today, the annual letters of thanks from the commanders can be viewed on the walls of the restaurants.

The tower in concrete construction since 1985

The border barriers in the eighties: vehicle path, automobile barrier ditch and metal lattice fence

Mounting of metal lattice mats, here between Apfelbach and Neuswarts

Signal fence

The opposition was also active in the eighties. Once again, the barriers, on which continual work was done, were changed. An automobile barrier ditch ran along behind the metal fencing, streams were piped or laid dry, uneven areas flattened, and the platoon path for repairs and control vehicles followed. The infamous self shooting systems disappeared; they were no longer needed because in the meantime a second fence approximately 500 meters Eastwards – the signal or rear fence – and been erected. The special feature was that it was equipped with weak current cables which, upon contact, transmitted a signal to one of the command towers. From here a patrol was then sent to area. Upon entry of the patrol in the gap between signal fence and Western fence – the area was partly still used agriculturally – the electrical current was disconnected after correct identification, so that a gate could be opened. The apron in front of the Western fence was hardly ever entered. Thorn bushes and small trees grew here. Overcoming the East fence unnoticed was nearly impossible for the trespasser.

"The General Defense Plan" – 1981

The military expansion was urgently necessary, because starting in 1981 in accordance with the "General Defense Plan" (GDP) the functions of the 11th Armored Cavalry Regiment were specified and increased. This plan, prepared by NATO and laid out with the highest security classification, nevertheless fell into the hands of the State Security Service and is accessible for viewing in the files of the state security service for everyone today. It shows in a terrifying fashion, which fate had been planned for our region through the feared attack.

The concept of frontal defense remained but the direction of attack of the aggressor was now considered to be the line Eisenach-Hersfeld–Alsfeld or Eisenach-Hünfeld-Schlitz; both cases north around Vogelsberg and no longer through Fulda and Kinzigtal. Whether this was correct, we do not know, since the Soviet plans of attack are not available. Two statements however seem to verify that the direction of attack on Fulda had not been given up. The Bishop of Fulda, Johannes Dyba, reported years after the reunification that the Russian Colonel General Burlakow, during the departure of his troops from Germany, told him he wanted to come to Fulda again. This city had been drawn as the main target on their map and had been selected as headquarters. This statement is supported by the former Mayor of Fulda, Dr. Wolfgang Hamberger, who reported that on 10 October 1992 the commander of the 8th Soviet Guard Army confirmed that Fulda was the attack target.

Within a strip of 50 kilometers behind the border – so the GDP – the aggressor should be stopped and smashed. The Blackhorse Regiment had the task of detaining the opponent approximately 24 hours in the control area as closely as possible behind the border. The 5th Corps would then attack. In order to manage this, and in addition to the purely military measures, further detainments were held ready. Nearly all roads were supplied with barriers, pits of six meters depth loaded with explosives which were to be ignited upon approach of the tanks. The resulting crater would have been so deep that if a tank drove into it, it could not get out again. Close to Point Alpha, on the narrow road to the hotel "Felsenkeller", there is such a pit to be seen. Today it belongs to the memorial Point Alpha – a board refers to its history. These pit covers are easily distinctive from the sewer drain covers because of the iron cross on the lid. Since several pits were always laid one behind the other, getting through would have been hindered. Ammunition and explosives were stored in "barrier supply houses" – small bunkers hidden in the forest, which would have been used in case of danger. In view of this awareness, one must ask, what would have happened to the civilian population in that strip, if there the opponent had had to be stopped and destroyed. There was little said about this in the plan. For the civilian population the slogan "Stay Put" was used; literally translated: stay where you've been put. One can imagine what fate they would have had; it would have been totally clear if nuclear weapons had been implemented. This was also taken into account in the plan; that is to say, if the conventional weapons could not stop the opponent. If an endangered unit requested "nuclear fire support" from central command, it could have been accomplished in 90 minutes. The plan shows nothing over the quantity and strength of the nuclear weapons. In 1976, in a first publication of an American text book on tactics, the peace research found a

Cover of the explosion pit on the entrance roads to Point Alpha

plan which was set to take place in Fulda.

In order to cause the opponent lasting casualties in the notorious triangle Hersfeld-Alsfeld- Fulda and down to Schweinfurt, the use of 141 „conventional" nuclear weapons would have been necessary (operation Zebra). A map shows that approximately ten would have been set up in the area of Vacha-Buttlar-Eiterfeld. Still more tightly meshed, they would have hit the referred to triangle, whereby the city of Fulda was left out. Rasdorf is labeled as target; the fate of Point Alpha would have been sealed. Even if this map is the result of a speculated scenario, it is nevertheless possible to imagine what would have happened to our area. The importance of Point Alpha is urgently represented in the informative and equally oppressive film, commentated by Peter Ustinov which is shown in a museum. Point Alpha, even if no nuclear weapons had been used, would have suffered

the following fate. It would have been informed of the approach by radio traffic in good time and it would have been able to observe it for awhile. However, the weak base would have been no more than a small pebble in the path of the aggressors. Lieutenant colonel Steven Steiniger expressed it later in an interview in such a way: "We did not have much ... we would have gotten the first alarm ... we knew that many of us would not survive." Although the encounter never took place, the memorial stone for the American soldiers on the Camp dedicated by the Point Alpha Memorial in 2000, was erected with full validity. Those soldiers serving duty there were constantly aware of the danger in which they lived.

The Soviet armed forces, whose attack was feared, were not stationed directly behind the border, but rather in sections of Meiningen or Gotha, approximately 40 or 60 kilometers away from Point Alpha.

Lieutenant Colonel Steven Steininger during his duty on Point Alpha

Memorial Stone with the inscription "To the US Tanker Reconnaissance Regiment 11th and 14th as thanks for their service for Peace and Freedom."

The troops belonged to 8th Guard Army, whose staff was situated in Weimar. In Meiningen, the 117th motorized infantry regiment was stationed along with: a battle tank unit, artillery on self-propelled gun carriage, an antitank defense unit, and a flier defense unit. This garrison accommodated approximately 350,000 soldiers in various barracks. However, only about ten kilometers from Point Alpha the 714 meters high „Baier" mountain north of Dermbach was periodically filled with Russian monitoring units. A larger, continuously occupied monitoring unit was already created north-west of Meiningen in the sixties on the mountain Geba between Werra and Felda. 60 to 70 soldiers, partially with families, were located here and operated their radar systems on their tracked vehicles. Their primary task was the monitoring of the radio traffic of the Americans on the Wasserkuppe. The helicopters for

the border control also started from the peak of Geba. Further east on the Dolmar, on the other side of the Werra, were the next rocket batteries with their range of up to 50 kilometers. The extensive training ground served also as shooting range for tanks. The American troops never came into contact with the Russians; Russian officers were seen only now and then in the border area.

Civil Rights Movement – Border Opening – 1985–1989

Fortunately it did not go any further than the planning games. The decay of the Soviet Union, the peaceful revolution in the GDR and the departure of the Soviet troops from Germany made further strategic considerations redundant. This surprising change in world politics did not come suddenly. It was initiated by the decision of the new Soviet leadership, under Michail Gorbatschow, to grant the citizens starting in 1985 a certain amount of participation and insight. Glasnost and Perestroika were the key words. Certainly these rights were quite modest. One could select among various candidates for the offices of management. But, it was shown that the Soviet system was reformable. Already in the next year it was shown that the satellite states had only been waiting for this signal, in order to likewise grant citizens participation rights. In 1988, in the CSSR, Poland and Hungary, citizen rights forums were created, and engaged citizens developed reform suggestions. In the GDR however, none of this was noticeable. Also here informal citizen rights groups had come together since 1984 – usually on the basis of the church bound peace movement –, but their participation in Government was unthinkable. Only exiting the country was now increasingly allowed. In 1988, approximately 3,000 migrants per month were counted, also visitors, certainly only individuals, were generously allowed to go to the West. When in May 1989 local elections took place, these citizen rights groups controlled the counting and revealed that the official numbers were falsified. In summer holidays, which the GDR inhabitants could as usual spend in the socialist brother countries, the urge to leave the country, took the upper hand: Hungary opened the border to Austria in July. There was no more holding them back; thousands fled out of the holiday areas to the border crossings and finally arrived in the Federal Republic. In Prague and Warsaw the holiday-makers pushed into the West German Embassy and finally achieved permission for their departure. The trip led straight through the middle of the GDR! But the civil rights activists had other goals;

they remained in the GDR and demanded reforms. The church peace prayers, which we had taken place already for many years, turned into enormous demonstrations for participation and civil liberties. At the end of September, individual groups, equal to parties, formally registered themselves and were accepted. The reform forces collected in the "new forum", the "democratic decampment" and the "social-democratic party", the later SPD. In October, the Monday peace demonstrations brought a hundred thousand people into the streets in Leipzig and Berlin. They shouted "We are the people!". The Government did not dare to intervene by force. The Political office arranged the resignation of Erich Honecker, discussions with the citizen rights groups were offered, and the entire Government finally withdrew. On 9 November, it was announced that the sector boundary in Berlin as well as the zone border could be crossed without a visa. In the same night, hordes of ecstatic people set out in West Berlin. A visit in the West – a first huge dream had gone into fulfillment. In our area the development took place with a certain delay. On 23 October, a first peace service was held in Geisa; on 6 November already 1,500 people had come together. Out of the surrounding villages the people streamed into the church in Geisa. Whoever was not able to come placed candles in the windows. A "round table" was formed in the cultural center in Geisa at which the responsible persons had to answer for their actions.

At the German domestic border it remained quiet on the night 9 November 1989. One could also cross the border to the West, but that was only possible at the previous crossing in Herleshausen and Eussenhausen. Long car queues formed. The call for further entrances to the border became more urgent. Already on Sunday, 12 November, the bridge near Vacha was opened, but the opening of B 84 from Rasdorf to Buttlar dragged on. The negotiations were lead by the BGS with the border troops of the GDR. Road building companies had to be engaged, in order to make the destructed road passable. Finally, on Sunday, 19 November, it could be opened. Already at 6 o'clock in the morning, a waiting group had forced the premature opening. The Eiterfeld music band was there as a greeting committee. The stream of visitors poured out mainly in direction west. In the meantime the wish for still more connections had become ever stronger; each village wanted to have at least one pedestrian crossing to the neighboring village. Angered citizens pushed their way through the countryside fence to the first fence and prepared to open the next

Preparation for opening the border on the B84 between Rasdorf and Buttlar

gate. Here the "Grenzers" (East German border patrols) took control, and finally, in most cases, they granted the opening for a few hours. Undergrowth, which had spread in the meantime in the apron and between the fences, had to be eliminated. Transitions between most localities had been created at the beginning of December in this way. However, the visa fee still had to be paid. Without control, crossing was impossible. On 8 December, the federal highway in the Ulstertal between Günthers and Motzlar was released.

The barriers had lost their authorization. The general desire was to tear down the hated fences as soon as possible. This was taken over by interested citizens who dismantled the fencing on their own and put it to practical use as garden or pasture fencing. In addition, the destruction desire raved against the surveillance towers, the gates and the electrical

On the B84 after the opening in November 1989
Luggage inspection at the border crossing

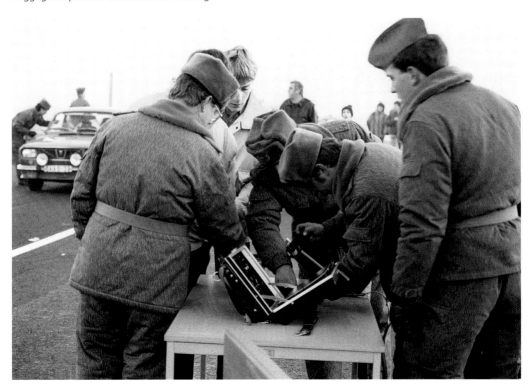

installations on the countryside fence. The border troops of the GDR arranged the systematic disassembly; heavy equipment had to tear the concrete piles out of the earth. A few years dragged on in the search for remaining mines. Then, only the vehicle paths proved witness of the former border between the two world powers.

For the occupation troops there were also no more tasks; neither the border control nor the defense of the Federal Republic. On 11 March, 1990, the Americans ended the border observation; Point Alpha was cleared out and closed. The locations in Fulda, Hersfeld and Kissingen were dissolved, the Blackhorse regiment returned to the USA.

Scar in the landscape: the border

US soldiers present a flag to a representative of the memorial place Point Alpha

48

From Asylum Hostel to Learning Place of History as of 1991

The Foundation is laid – 1991–2000

What happened to Point Alpha after the departure of the Americans? The area changed hands and became the possession of the Federal Republic. They planned its renaturation – the re-integration into nature – which would have meant the demolition of the buildings and ripping up of the concrete paving. It was also considered using the area as a construction stock pile. But it did not come to that. The artist association "rainbow" under its leader Josef Knecht had already before the peaceful revolution attempted to mount a work of art at the border; a 50 meter long rainbow made of steel and stretching over the border. Later, they decorated the command tower at Wiesenfeld with a multicolored rainbow. The funds were not enough however for the implementation of the ambitious art project. The group had to stop their efforts in July 1994. Meanwhile, in summer 1992, asylum-seekers had been quartered into the three barracks. They lived there up to the spring of 1995. Once again the area stood uninhabited and a welcome object of destruction for several unknown people. They cut open the fence, destroyed windows and doors and even damaged the roofs so that the rain came in. The barracks were no longer habitable; the area only debris.

In the meantime citizens from Rasdorf and Geisa had set the goal, under the direction of Berthold Dücker, to preserve and to set up a warning, memorial and meeting

place. The Free State Thuringia had already financed the preservation of a part of the metal grid fence in 1993. Now an association had to be formed, because only then was the Free State Thuringia ready to invest further funds into the project. In July 1995, the association "border museum Rhoen Point Alpha registered association", was formed with its seat in Rasdorf/Hesse. The principal purpose was to hinder the renaturation and to preserve the unit of the American Armed Forces as singular monument of the recent German history for future generations. In 1997, the Thuringia parallel association, with its seat in Geisa, was

Barrack A (top) and Barrack C (bottom) after the closing of the Asylum Hostel

49

formed for sponsorship reasons. The two associations always decided things together. The historically significant point should be a warning to always hinder the dangerous confrontation of two world powers; it should be a reminder of the unjust State GDR and of the constricting barriers and should enable the meeting of young people, who could get together in this surrounding context to exchange on political issues. The place is particularly suitable for it. One is in an open, free landscape, which offers a view into the two formerly separated regions and one stands in front of a military leftover of the Cold War, where everyone feels that they are standing on historical pregnant ground. Whoever thinks of the border or of the duty of the soldiers stationed here, must inevitably sense a feeling of embarrassment and compassion.

In order to carry out their ideas, it was however first necessary to receive funding for the project. The association managed to win the Thuringia state parliament delegates Dr. Hans-Peter Häfner and his Hessian colleague Winfried Rippert for the plan. Also the mayors von Rasdorf and Geisa as well as the district administrator of the Wartburg district, Dr. Martin Kaspari, supported them immediately. But while Dr. Häfner encountered rapid agreement and funding possibilities in his Government, this was not the case in Hesse. The Hessian nature protection did finally give up the renaturation plan. The Thuringian Prime Minister Dr. Bernhard Vogel could be convinced of the project. 1995, in the founding year, he had come for a visit.

For 1996 funds were made available. With a meeting of the Prime

Visit of Prime Minister Dr. Bernhard Vogel (from left: MdI Rippert, Prime Minister Vogel, B.Dücker, and Mayor Körbel)

Ministers Dr. Bernhard Vogel and Hans Eichel in the next year, Hesse conceded to at least check the sponsor worthiness; the museum fund should not give any aid though. Nevertheless, the area was now under monument protection, no changes could be made; the first major success of the sponsor associations of Point Alpha.

Berthold Dücker knew how to keep the site alive in the memories by inviting prominent personalities; as he did for the annual celebration hours for the day of the German reunion. In November 1996, the former commander of the Blackhorse regiment, now Chief of the 5th American Army Corps, Lieutenant General Abrams, visited the former US Camp. At the end of 1997 Winfried Rippert and Dr. Häfner, after repeated meetings in Kassel, were able to change the minds of the hesitant Hessian authorities so that they consented to an ABM measure (special measure for unemployed people) for 1998. The subsidies of

the country Thuringia had been used for the most important constructional problems of the barracks. In the year 1997 a caretaker moved into Barrack A so that further destruction was hindered.

In the meantime the members of the association had started to collect and mount exhibits for a permanent exhibition; equipment pieces and uniforms of the American troops. A model of the border installations was donated by the Federal Border Security (BGS), as well as a BGS helicopter; also two NVA vehicles were located in the former vehicle hanger. Work was done on "the example border", the original reproduction of the various units.

In summer 1998, in the renovated Barrack A, the permanent exhibition was opened, to which over 1,000 guests appeared. Special exhibitions in previous years had also been possible. When a CDU Government had been formed in Hesse in February 1999, the Prime Ministers Dr. Bernhard Vogel and Roland Koch met in

Aerial view in the year 1997 (Rudolf Karpe, Media Center, District and Communal Picture Pffice)

the summer of 1999 and ensured the employment of a managing director, a caretaker and of two typists as ABM measure.

Now Barrack B with accommodation for young people could also be tackled; in the same way, Barrack C was set up with a cafeteria for the ever increasing flow of visitors. In the summer "a family day" had been organized with a children's program, in order to make further visitors familiar with the place. The educational work started in November 1999 with a history lesson for pupils of the 8th class from Geisa and Rasdorf in the group room of Barrack B, which the Secretaries of Cultural Affairs from Hesse and Thuringia attended. With all of this, the entire spectrum of the projects had unfolded after only five years after the foundation of the association.

Further Development – 2000–2003

This basis demanded expansion and widening. The year 2000 held three possibilities. In May, veterans of the 14th and 11th cavalry regiments joined together for a "reunion" in Fulda; A ceremony which naturally had to take place at Point Alpha.

Here, everything was the same, just as they remembered it, whereas in Fulda the Downs Barracks had long since gone to civil hands and was changed accordingly. During this event a memorial for the American soldiers who had defended freedom in Germany was erected and honored. Around 300 guests came, among them the previous Commander General Abrams and the Prime Minister Dr. Vogel. Larger public attention was given to the Ceremony of the "Memorial of the German Separation and Re-unification" on 13 August. There are two six meter

high wooden blocks which greet, just outside the camps of the previous border far into the Geisar country. The piece of art was created by wood working students of the occupational education center in Bad Salzungen. The speakers of the ceremony, the Prime Ministers Dr. Bernhard Vogel and Roland Koch, remembered the "Victims of the German Separation", the courageous and peaceful revolution of 1989, and the builders of the Reunification" (wording of the memorial salutation). The 10th anniversary of the Germany Unity on 3 October 2000 was begun with a two day celebration. Whereas the memory of 40 years of GDR ruling was paid service with devotion and ceremony, the second day was devoted to joy. Through music, pre-lunch drinks, children and family programs and evenings even with disco music, an atmosphere of a public party developed which attracted nearly 10,000 visitors. The entire event was made possible by a private sponsor, Mr. Werner Deschauer – a previous citizen of Geisa who lives with his wife Anneliese in Bochum. It was no wonder that the media was present and that Point Alpha appeared on the TV screen. That over all the years, all these meetings brought the places closer to the public is seen in the rising numbers of visitors, which rose from 30,000 to 60,000 in the year 2003. Not only did school classes arrive, but groups from totally different areas, chose Point Alpha as their meeting point, among them, also an increasing number of groups from foreign countries. The historical location radiates a stronger attraction than other museums. Thus devotions and wreathlaying took place here after the terrorist attack on 11 September 2001. The tours soon developed into regular discussion rounds so that the meeting character of the meeting place was more directly addressed. On the other side the administration had to manage the visitors. That was done primarily in 2001 via the transformation of the Cafeteria, and otherwise with the increase of the exhibition inventory. A powerful battle tank M 60 and an armored crew transporter M 113-A2 were donated by the US Armed Forces before the observation area of the tower was renovated. In the next years the accommodations could be finished in Barrack B. The association already had a further large-scale project in mind, for which substantially higher funds were required, i.e. a second and a larger exhibition building. But on the grounds of the post, where nothing could be changed, there was no room.

The House on the Border – 2003

The construction of the second exhibition building was a crucial step, in order to achieve the goal set by the association. Here the border regime of the GDR as well as the forced evacuations and the fate of the razed yards should be depicted. It was realized in 2003 and influenced this year. The desire for it must have arisen very soon in the association, because already in 1999 negotiations were said to have taken place with the nature protection authority on the building site on the platoon path, also in the Thuringian area. The plan was finalized and accepted in the general meeting 2000; also the biosphere reservation and the ideas of the "Green Strip" should be made descriptive in the "pavilion". In March of the next year, the dates for the commencement of construction and the opening were already on the assembly agenda … In August 2001, (building of the Wall in Berlin 40 years ago!),

the first cut of the spade was done symbolically. It took however still another year, until in April the property questions were clarified, in spring 2002 the Thuringian state gave the funding, and since donations from private people had likewise come in, the foundation could be laid. The construction began in August. It progressed rapidly. In October (day of the German Unity) the later German Chancellor Dr. Angela Merkel gave the commemorative speech to the building celebration. In December the framework construction was roofed. After spring, a new water pipeline had been laid up from Geisa; the opening – again on the historical date of the People's Uprising in 1953 – could be celebrated on 15 June 2003 in the presence of the Prime Minister Dieter

Topping-Out Ceremony on 3 October 2002 with Dr. Angela Merkel, the CDU-party Chairman

Althaus, his predecessor Dr. Bernhard Vogel and further Thuringian and Hessian cabinet members. Many broadcasters, also from outer regions, reported. At the opening all speakers described the "House on the border" as a museum on a historically important place and indeed "a learning place of history".

A double house of 17x13 and 24 meters respectively had resulted, painted blue and light-grey. The colors symbolized the European Union, whose funds had flowed, and the bluish-gray of the barracks of the observation Point Alpha. The house on the border was deliberately placed on the former death strip. The platoon path, which is under monument protection, runs straight through the middle of the large exhibition hall – a very impressive special feature. Project management was under the direction of the Thuringian "land development company". Local craftsmen carried out the work, a team of four with Dr. Matthias Schmidt from Fulda developed the museum design. In the smaller section a conference and presentation room was set up, in which special exhibitions could also take place. In the upper floor are the landscape panoramas, where animals and plants of the biosphere reservation can be seen. The volcanism of the Rhoen is brought close through a walk in "active volcano". Here the visitor can become active himself; producing the scream of a buzzard by pushing a button or observe insect larva through a microscope. From the roof terrace, the Ulstertal and the

Model of the Biosphere Reservation Rhoen in the House on the Border

Hes-
sian Kegelspiel
offer an impressive sight.
In the larger building, the visitor is confronted directly with the border barrier systems. Upon entering, the visitor comes face to face with the high metal grid fence and is inevitably confronted with the oppressive feeling of being imprisoned. If he looks upward for open spaces, he is limited on the right by a over-whelming grey surveillance tower with guards, to the left he loses himself in the Rhoen countryside with trees, heath, rocks, animals and even a stream with trout; however also here he sees guards, who emerge here and there – the border soldiers. The op-

pres-
sive atmosphere
does not become milder,
when, after having studied the boards on the separation of Germany, one goes along the border fence.

Here the individual phases of the closing of the frontier are documented; next to it, the expelling of the inhabitants close to the border in 1952, as well as the fate of the razed farmyards. The dangerous mines between the double fences lay ahead of us, a self shooting device threatens over head. Then one enters the divi-

Diorama "Kalkma-gerrasen" on the first floor of the House on the Border

The Round Table in front of the House on the Border

sion area of the border troops, with uniforms, equipment, testimonies of the soldiers and a commander area. Amongst them the escape attempts are documented, the shooting command explained, and some of the weapons and vehicles can be viewed. In two examples one shows, how the victims under the border troops were glorified. A film explains the division of Germany and the history of the GDR. Finally, going through a fence gate, one arrives as it were into freedom. Outside are parts of the Berlin wall – in a glass showcase – and a round wooden table with 16 stools for the 16 states of the Federal Republic, as remembrance of the days of the peaceful revolution in 1989. In nine meters height, an enormous and very symbolic metal spiral – created by the artist Friedel Deventer from Kassel and often photographed – turns in the air with the words "peace" written in German, English and Russian on its three wings.

The House on the Border with the Peace Spiral

Even More Offers - 2003–2005

With this exhibition, logically new tasks came to the association. Through the depiction of the barriers, the forced evacuations, the escapes and the border incidents in the exhibition buildings, arose the visitors' need to see these places in their natural settings. The example border was for many too sterile. One had already been trying to meet this need for many years; the Rhoen Club in

Geisa had occupied itself since 2000 with a system of a 17 km long didactic exhibition along the border, which extends from Wenigentaft over Point Alpha up into Geisa.

The development was continually worked on; 19 boards at important points explain the special characteristics of the areas. They were able to open it punctually for the house inauguration in April 2003. However, trained guides were needed for both the didactic exhibition along the border as well as for the exhibition itself. This had also been planned for in good time. Since the beginning of the year, recruiting for this had taken place. The recruits learned the historical and command-technical basics in 70 lessons. In July, 19 trained guides were introduced, who then carried out more than 500 guided tours in the year 2004.

In a completely different area the association tried to attract visitors, through artistic events in or outside the former Camp. In August 2003, for the first time, the lecturer-artist Rudolph H. Herget appeared, and presented an evening poet reading under the title "Overcoming Borders – and Then There Was Light". This was repeated several times over the next years. Surely, the place in front

Opening of the Learning Path along the Border at Buchenmühle in April 2003

The Alphornbläser "Siebenschläfer" from Geisa at the Benefit Concert 2005

Police Music Corps Thuringia and National Police Orchestra Hesse at the Benefit Concert 2005

of the tower with its wide view also contributed to the success of this offer. Another innovation came with the former vehicle hanger. Here various music groups from the surrounding communities gathered to present a concert program. The police music corps from Thuringia and Hesse played in benefit of a hostel for parents of children cancer victims in Jena and Frankfurt a. Main. Since then yearly benefit programs take place in co-operation with the local clubs.

A third support was the theater performances. The first took place in September 2004 in the House on the Border. Two actors agreed to perform; the married couple Nedelmann from "Independent Eisenach Citizens Theater". After a children's performance, they performed "Klamms Krieg", the history of a teacher, who had to fight against unfair accusation of guilt. The following regular theater performances had to be limited to two roles. The repertoire of the two consists to a large extent of personal productions, which describe the life in the GDR, e.g. "Born in the GDR".

The most ambitious goal of the association, the transfer of a historical consciousness to young people, came closer only slowly. The possibilities were limited first to one-day seminars, to which the Hessian "HeLP" – an advanced training organization for teachers – was invited. In July a theater project, which was offered under the title "History Brought to the POINT", was accomplished. An 8th grade class from Bad Liebenstein was interactively confronted with the separation of Germany and the consequences thereof. The children were able to present

Benefit Concert 2005. The patrons of the two countries Hesse and Thuringia Volker Bouffier and Dr. Karl Heinz Gasser in discussion with Police Director Raimond Walk and the Chairman of the Board of the Border Museum Rhoen "Point Alpha" Berthold Dücker

*At the presenta-
tion of the project
"Life before 1989
on Both Sides of
the Border"*

their experiences in a live scene sequence. They were advised and
coached for it by the two actors. In
autumn 2005, a research project
with high school class pupils from
Vacha and Hünfeld had started. Under the title "Life before 1989 on
Both Sides of the Border", they tried
to collect as much information and
knowledge as possible through
source studies and interviews over a
period of a year in their spare time.
This collection was then to be presented in a film. Accompanying this
were work shops which lasted several
days with overnight accommodation
on the Point Alpha. The entire project was sponsored by the community colleges (Volkshochschulen) of
the districts of Fulda and Wartburg.
The project was nominated for the
German Unity Prize.

In addition, the annual celebrations, which had already become tradition, took place; the family days,
the ceremonies on 17 June, 13 August and 2nd and 3rd of October, as
well as many meetings of the most
diverse groups: journalists, entrepre-
neurs, veterans. A delegation of the
two US regiments stationed in Fulda
had also organized a wide scoped
commemoration ceremony in 2005.
All of this was overwhelmed by larg-

*Scene of the thea-
tre project "History
Brought to the
Point"*

er events. The award of the "German Unity prize"/"Citizen Award" took place on 2 October 2004 in Erfurt in connection with the official celebrations of the German Unity Day. However, it demonstrated that the memorial place had become popular on the Federal level. This prize, awarded the first time in 2002, was donated by the Federal Head Office for Political Education and could be given to initiates who were active in the "Development of the German Domestic Unity". The award speech for the winner Point Alpha was held by Prime Minister Dieter Althaus.

Three weeks prior an important historical event on Point Alpha had been celebrated; the border opening between Hungary and Austria, which precipitated the fall of the wall 15 years earlier. Thousands of East Germans, who had spent their vacation in Hungary, were at that time able to travel into the West. The association administration had succeeded in inviting two high-ranking politicians who, at that time, had made the opening possible; the previous German Minister of Foreign Affairs, Hans Dietrich Genscher, and his Hungarian colleague Gyula Horn. They met for a celebration and a round of talks. Since a youth camp with German and Hungarian participants was in progress at the same time, the young people had the opportunity to see first hand the preparations and the meaning of this first step towards the opening. In a panel discussion, the two Ministers of Foreign Affairs chatted openly about their experiences. Several hundred guests populated the area between the House on the Border and the former Camp.

Memorial Celebration 2004 in memory of the opening of the border between Hungary and Austria. From left: The former Federal Foreign Minister Hans-Dietrich Genscher, an interpreter, Thuringian Prime Minister Dieter Althaus, the former Hungarian Foreign Minister Gyula Horn and the Mayor of Geisa Peter Günter

Point Alpha Prize – 2005

In the year 2005, a plan could be carried out, on which the association chairman Berthold Dücker himself had already begun working in 2003; to award a prize to personalities with exceptional "services in the Unity of Germany and Europe in Peace and Liberty". A curator had formed for this, which the former Thuringian Federal State Parliament President Christine Lieberknecht headed. In May 2005, the media also announced the persons selected for the "Point Alpha Prize": Michail Gorbatschow, George Bush sr. and Dr. Helmut Kohl, all statesmen of

Ceremony of the awarding of the "Point Alpha Prize" on 17 June 2005 in front of the House on the Border on the previous death strip

first rank. In the following weeks new details of the meeting, which was scheduled for Friday the 17th June 2005, the anniversary of the People's Uprising, were regularly announced. It was a ceremony including the transfer of models of the Unity Monument and a "Trialogue" between the three politicians, who could then afterwards join the celebration. Over 10,000 visitors were expected, 5 TV stations provided transmission, and 180 journalists had announced themselves, supported by 70 technicians. 1,200 policemen, partially in civilian clothes, should guarantee safety. A special attraction was the flight of three domesticated eagles; the coat of arms animals of the USA, Russia and Germany. At the House on the Border, the prize winners were given a roofed area and the events were transmitted on a large screen. After six speakers for the honoring of the prize winners were found in the last minute – people from sport, art, science, economics and the chairman Dücker himself – the event took place under good weather and no incidents.

Not only was Point Alpha to be seen on all channels, attaining thereby international recognition, but it was also offered Federal funding for the future – a desire that up to then had only been presented in vain. At the end of the year, 90,000 visitors had been counted – 30,000 more than the previous year.

Group Photo after the award of the "Point Alpha Prize". From left: Christine Lieberknecht, President of the Curator German Unity, Award Winner George Bush senior, Award Winner Dr. Helmuth Kohl, Hessian Prime Minister Roland Koch, Thuringian Prime Minister Dieter Althaus and Award Winner Michail Gorbatschow

The Research Project is Completed – 2006

Evening readings showed a remarkable shift in topic in the year 2006. The oppression methods in the GDR were recalled and at the same time the current tendency to "play down" and make the state observation harmless was revealed as a dangerous falsifying of history by Bärbel Bohly and Ingrid Vitzthum, through Grafe's reports on processes against marksmen at the border and Schreiber's book "Im Visier" ("In Sight"). Each time the hall was overfilled. It was no different as the first symposium on the German Domestic Border with renowned scientists and time-witnesses, which had been organized by the Hessian Institute for Political Education at the beginning of 2007.

The earlier mentioned research project, which had begun in September 2005, was now completed after one year. The two community colleges of the districts of Fulda and Wartburg had received the necessary funds from the Federal Children and Youth Plan. Thirteen girls and seven boys from the upper classes of the Vacha and Hünfeld High School could now occupy themselves for one year with the topic "Life before 1989 on Both Sides of the Border". They studied the literature, the asked time-witness and specialists and recorded their results in reports. They were advised and directed by experts during this unusual work. In weekend meetings held monthly on Point Alpha they compared and examined their results. This all took place outside of school time. On 14 September 2006, the results were publicly presented. Not only had the representatives of the community college spoken at the presentation, but also those of the Ministries of Education and Culture. They underlined the uniqueness of the work, since it had united young people from East and West and at the same time had documented the way of life for the residents on the mutual border. In nearly 50 contributions the pupils had processed various topics; primarily the forced evictions of 1952, and 1961 and later, a topic which came too short in GDR history. Contributions from the everyday life came in second place, followed by the reports on successful escapes. The individual stations of the fortification of the border and its opening had not been forgotten; members of Border Security (BGS) of border troops also talked about their service. The power of the party and the public security became once again clearer and clearer. The results were presented in the celebration hour by the individual teams in the form of reports, illustrations, scenic representations, and particularly impressive through a short theater piece on the forced eviction. Experienced teachers and aids helped with the presentations and the media processing of CDs and DVDs. All speakers declared that with this project on the GDR the devastating knowledge gaps could be filled. The Point Alpha team had thus fulfilled its goals in an ideal fashion.

Reading in January 2006 with Bärbel Bohley and Ingrid Vitzthum, Moderator Gerald Praschl

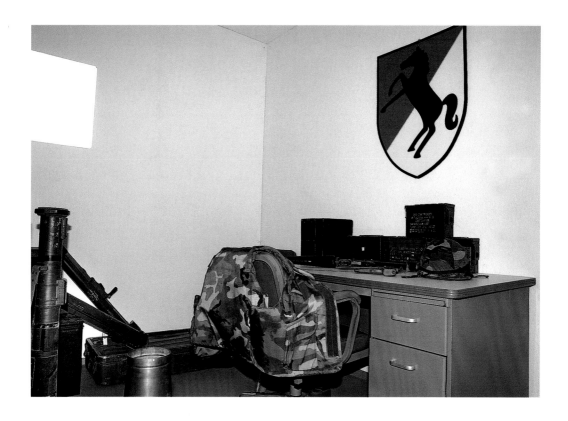

New Exhibition in the US Camp – 2007

The prerequisites for another upcoming task had been already established in 2006; the reorganization of the exhibition on the western side of the border which had to find its place in the former US Camp. Funds for it had been allocated by the Federation, which together with a Hessian funding, enabled the contract for the concept development. The plan was presented in September 2006. In contrast to the House on the Border, the museum-educational possibilities were limited by the existing premises. Barrack A, the only available building, was narrow and became even narrower due to a hallway in the middle of the exhibition area. The visitors are first conducted to the left. This approximately thirty meters long room can be crossed only in one direction. This is where the entire history of the American Armed Forces in Hesse since 1945 is to be represented – naturally most importantly the occupation of Point Alpha up to the departure of the troops in 1990. For the understanding of the exhibits shown here, a time track is essential on which the most important political changes in this half century are specified. This takes place on the right by means of short texts and illustrations, with picture windows, which the visitor can open as well as with drawers with explanatory texts. At some desks faces of "time-witnesses" appear on a monitor by pushing a button and their reports can be heard on a head set. Opposite this time track, memoranda of the respective American troops, who did

Exhibition in the previous ammunitions bunker

service at the border, is displayed in showcases. The question "What happened back then?" should be answered through this exhibition. The various equipment, weapons and traditional items are completed by illustrations of the daily duty at the border. Affected were the Constabulary Units, then 14th and the 11th Armored Cavalry Regiment. Amongst other "time-witnesses", desks are available at which films can be watched on a monitor with head set, as well as drawers with illustrations and texts for study. A special audio-visual equipped "Station" describes the duty on Point Alpha after 1972, when one feared a Soviet attack at the Fulda Gap. The strategic considerations of this time are clarified in a panorama. Finally, the relations between the Americans and the Federal Border Security, Customs and the German population are referred to. As tour conclusion, the visitor experiences, how after the border opening and the departure of the troops, the military camp was transformed into the current Warning, Memorial and Meeting place. The highlight is the audio-visual playback of the ceremonies for the award of the Point Alpha prize in 2005. Now the visitor leaves the showroom and arrives by way of the hallway outside. Here however the visitor encounters a surprise; life-size photos of American soldiers standing at attention flank the hall on the right and left. The visitor look them straight in the face. The idea is to show that the soldiers in formation appeared as a mass, in reality however they were individuals with whom one could communicate. Before exiting, the visitor can have a look at the accommodation space and dormitories of the soldiers, which appears to have been only recently left by its inhabitants. Outside one is en-

compassed by nature and the trees which experienced those times; those times which were the laborious cause of the exhibition. Descriptive explanations of the situation from 1945 to 1989, with special attention to the US Camp Point

Alpha, are given on large boards. Diverse objects such as military vehicles, helicopters, and tents etc. round off the presentation impressively.

Step by step and extremely carefully, under the direction of histori-an and museum experts, the area is returned to its original state; as far as that is possible and reasonable. Regrettably, very much was destroyed or disappeared during transfer of the real estate to the association.

Former guarded gate entrance of Point Alpha

*Exhibition of US
military vehicles
on the grounds of
earlier observation
base*

We are the people! Are we a people?

Speech of Dr. Wolfgang Hamberger, Mayor retired of Fulda, at Point Alpha,
2. October 2005

In this place, where so many memories overwhelm me, I do not find it easy to balance rational and emotion. **Therefore, I am extraordinarily grateful to Berthold Dücker that he saved the historical place OP Alpha and made a warning, memorial and a meeting place out of it. Through this, an unbelievably important contribution against forgetting has been made for all times.** With all respect for the landscape: here no nature protection was needed but rather that needed to be protected which realistically documents the German Division and offers coming generations at least an idea of what the Cold War, in its perceptible confrontation in this place, meant for the world. Finally, not only two modern armies equipped with the best weapon systems aligned themselves here, but also to two entirely different world views: Liberty and human rights on the one side, spying, monitoring, terror and pursuit on the other side. We also owe it to our American friends to remember. Seen like this, Point Alpha is today a place with great symbolic energy, a lasting visible proof of freedom's victory over all tyranny. Thank God and the Americans!

Everything that has been achieved with so much dedication and energy by the Association Border Museum Rhoen "Point Alpha" registered association – founded by Berthold Dücker – is great. But with all due acknowledgment of the financial help that was exemplarily contributed from the outset by the state of Thuringia and with a certain delay also provided by the state of Hesse, I wish – actually it should be demanded – that the Federation would acknowledge the national importance of this place and provide institutional funding. Because I am realist enough; an association can accomplish a great deal with its honorary commitment and the material assistance of its members, but if it is to be permanently responsible for the running costs of an actually national concern and must appear everywhere as petitioner, even the highest energy will sooner or later become lame. This may never be allowed to happen!

In 1989 the call sounded: "We are the people", and today, in the space of the years, we must place this encouraging avowal as a critical question: "Are we a people?" I formulate this deliberately in a kind of provocative manner in order to remind, in order to energize, to not simply take notice but rather to reflect and recall to our memories what we experienced and how it felt, in order to be able to assess, with this as a background, whether I outlined the historical process correctly and in the sense of individual memories.

1. The Prehistory, the Event,
the Evaluation

What it was that moved the people in the GDR before the so-called "Wende" ("Turning Point") and brought them with unbelievable courage to the streets did not begin first in 1989. On the contrary, there is a long prehistory. Do not forget the bloodily crushed national uprising of 17 June 1953! On this day a political signal with long-term effect was given. Do not forget those approximately 1,000 Wall-deaths! Do not forget the many, who were incarcerated in Bautzen and other prisons because of their desire for liberty and for standing up for human rights! Do not forget those, who, as also in the case of Berthold Dücker, under the highest mortal danger, succeeded in their adventurous escape! What courage one must have, what a strong will, in order to escape a fate, from which, measured against the norm, no escape was possible! All those like Berthold Dücker, who took up this daring venture became important admonishers in the Federal Republic. They reported their bitter experiences. And, when politicians threatened to succumb to the temptation of treating something, which was abnormal, as a fateful given, to resign and accept the Division of Germany and began to say, one must see the hard facts soberly and accept reality, they shook them awake again. The fundamental agreement to never accept the German Division as a permanent condition had become for many, who thought the relative security of the Federal Republic was an understood, endangered with time. This danger was averted in the end by those, who had experienced, and had suffered the real existing socialism and turned their backs on it. Those, who one adversely insulted in the GDR as "fugitives of the republic", became the conscience of the whole German nation in the Federal Republic!

Hungary 1956 and Prague 1968 may not be forgotten! The pictures of Prague in spring, when the People's Army units of the GDR invaded, have burned themselves deep in my memory. The communist system still seemed strong, the inhibition to be a part of it when, before the eyes of the entire world, brutal force was used against human, was still very low and we in the west became helpless observers of a tragedy which, without the protection of the Americans, could have also become our own fate. Nevertheless, the courageous citizens of Prague wanted nothing more than a little more breathing space for a dignified way of life.

Do not forget the man who – the clearing up of the past will at some point show it – made an unbelievably important contribution to the development; Pope John Paul ll. His vast authority, his absolute trustworthiness, his unshaken demand for human rights and his deep love of God and the people were important impacts and strong forces in a process which became more and more dynamic until it was no longer to be stopped. Beginning at that time, when this Pope traveled for the first time to his Polish homeland to bring the people his message and to show the government its limits – at the latest on this day – those in power in the communistic blocks understood that they no longer could do what ever they wanted to. Because with this Pope, a man had come onto to the stage who was not only acknowledged as a moral authority world wide, whose effectiveness was accompanied and closely observed every step of the way by the international public, but also a man who instead of diplomatically formulating, argued politically. The answer to the once posed sardonic question from Stalin: "How many battalions does the Pope have?" could not have not been more appropriate.

We should also not forget that the GDR stood just before its national economical collapse in autumn of 1989; even if the SED functionaries suppressed it and the West did not want to believe it. When the statistics are manipulated year for year, the statisticians themselves no longer know which numbers are correct. That is not too amazing, but I still wonder today that in Bonn a well staffed all German Ministry existed over decades and nevertheless at the time of the „Wende" no-one was prepared to give all German answers.

If we ask the people today, not only those who live in Thuringia, in the Wartburg district or in Hesse – Fulda or Rasdorf – but also those who live where the border awareness could not become so true to life as with us, for example in the Rhineland, what they remember about the German Unity, most likely most of them will say – the fall of the Berlin Wall on 9 November 1989. This is the deepest and impressive emotional memory of all Germans. But, the peaceful revolution began earlier! Not only the Wall birds from 1989, but also the citizens of the GDR, who started the "Wende" process under the motto "Destined for Freedom", are architects of the German Unity. Already in spring 1989, using all their courageous desperation, they demanded the democratic renewal of society on their pamphlets, held the SED, People's Police and Stasi in check and prepared the autumn of 1989. Here only a few facts: In Leipzig, on 15 January 1989, 500 citizens demanded freedom of opinion, assembly and freedom of the press. 53 of them were "added" as was termed in the harmless jargon of the system and which in fact meant that they were arrested and sent to the next prison. That was reality; that was the answer from the apparatus to the call of freedom and self-regulation. But, the functionaries began to feel that this concept of taking action was slipping through theirs fingers, they recognized that the international press never let them out of their sight and they felt that history would necessarily take its course. **The Monday peace prayers in the Leipzig Nikolaikirche became the signal for the entire country. I can only repeat with admiration and great respect: these people risked everything and gave the world proof of the best citizen spirit!**

Then, fate took its course. At the communal elections on 7 May 1989, for the first time, it was possible to prove that the SED had falsified the election counts and this led to more and more people disassociating themselves with the system, even if not everyone admitted it openly. Whoever sat fearfully at home, is not to be condemned – the human temperament does not let everyone hear the calling of martyrdom – but, those who in full knowledge of the danger, overcame their inner resistance, and openly proclaimed and decisively demonstrated in the streets, must be admired for all times to come.

Soon the events were rushing on. On 10 September 1989 Gyula Horn ripped a hole in the Iron Curtain and everyone who had come to the Pan European Union, seized the opportunity and chose the way to freedom; there was no holding them back. One has to put himself in the position of these people in order to understand, or at least have a vague idea, what had happened: at home, everything left where it was, a rushed departure with no goodbyes, leaving the holiday area in one of GDR neighbouring countries, head over heals

with a totally unknown goal, always in a panicky fear they might come too late, driven only by the chance of gaining their freedom. What courageous and fantastic people they were!

On 3 October 1989 the Dresden People's Police and the National People's Army took brutal action against all those who tried to jump on the trains coming out of Prague, which the Regime – a ridiculous case of political misjudgment – had allowed to drive through the GDR. I will never forget the 5 October. I was notified in my office in the morning that at 11:00, 11:20 and 12:00 trains from Prague would be arriving at the Fulda train station and that we had to provide the people with food, beverages and all other necessary items. The unbelievable was before us: unique hours in which history was made, moving moments, exciting encounters! My colleagues in the administration supported by business people, and a few volunteers organized everything within the shortest time, and then we all stood punctually on the platform ready and waiting. What an experience! We just had to provide for the GDR refugees in the trains, they however made us richer through letting us feel some of their unimaginable courage as they shouted out their joy and transmitted their hopes and faith in a better future and by assuring us of finally being on the right side now. Again and again they unified with the cry – Freedom! Freedom! – in a unison chorus, a true outcry, so penetrant and loud, as if they wanted it to carry and be heard on the other side of the border. Many of them gave us their address and asked us to use our return address and to write to their families at home to let them know that one or the other of them had made it: **Write them that we are in the West, that we have Freedom; that's enough!** Can anyone forget something like this?

At the time I had three visiting American journalists in the town hall who wanted get to know something about German communal administration. I involved them in this action as well and told them that they would now get a chance to experience history in the making. All three of them were deeply moved, affected, committed and full of energy. "Unbelievable" was the word they used most. No clever argument, or comment, and no documentation could have convinced them more how important it is to fight with all your energy for freedom and peace.

The 7 October 1989 will remain an unparalleled memory for many of us. In Berlin the SED staged a ghostly celebration for the 40th year of the founding of the GDR and documented with it their total loss of reality. While the old men in the Political Offices embraced, kissed and drank toasts to their supposed socialistic achievements, the people chanted in front of the Republic Palace "Gorbi Help!" Mielke, the Stasi omnipotent, demanded hard and unyieldingly the end of all humanism (not much later, he seemed to know nothing about this as he called to the Member of the People's Chamber, "I love you all!"). This was the macabre swan song of a long since faded time, the eve of a really new time. The SED functionaries did not notice anything anymore; they only had one goal, to cement their rule as long as possible. But, only two days later the decision fell. The operation location was Leipzig, the area in front of the Nikolaikirche, where 70,000 people peacefully demonstrated surrounded by 8,000 security officers! In the Leipzig People's Newspaper, the SED had threatened: "We are ready and willing, to effectively protect what we have accomplished, if needed, then with a weapon in our hands."
Would tanks arrive, would shots fall? Is the Chinese solution threatening? Fearful questions. Nobody knew if they would survive the next day. Who can distinguish between doubt and desperation, who knows the mortal fear of those many? A citizen's protest turned into a large scale fire. Four weeks later the end had arrived.

On 9 November 1989, the Iron Curtain broke and it needs to be stated: the Wall fell from East to West! It was not the freedom pampered West Germans who managed it; it was the GDR citizens who brought the Wall down. The pictures of the Trabi-caravans through Berlin, the joy at the Brandenburger Tor and the thrilled, dancing people on the Wall, will most likely remain for ever. As I arrived early in the morning in the town hall on 11th November to head off with my driver to an appointment outwards, 50 people from the GDR were standing in the courtyard to receive the 100 DM welcome money which the state had arranged. The Schabowski-Speech made us listen up and I had of course given orders on the previous evening, since we normally used cashless payment procedures, to make sure we had enough 100 Euro bills, but in this case what was enough? By late morning, thousands out of the GDR had arrived, by afternoon the city was completely clogged with trabis and within a matter of days, we had paid millions in welcoming money, money which we did not even have. Once again, the communal autonomy proved itself excellently.

The impressive, ecumenical devotion on the Domplatz at which thousands who had come from across the border took part, became the crowning final of this historical weekend on which a dream had come true. One week later, on 19 November, I climbed into a helicopter with the Regiment Commander of the 11th US Tanker Reconnaissance Regiment stationed in Fulda, Colonel John N. Abrams. We flew to Philippsthal and from there directly back over the border landing exactly on the street to Buttlar where a new Border crossing was being created. Unforgettable scenes were taking place there. A young soldier of the GDR Border Troop came hesitantly over to me and asked if he could have a look in the helicopter. Colonel Abrams allowed it and then the soldier said "You know, we recognize this helicopter from its silhouette, and the sounds of the blades, but I don't know much more". As he came back, astounded, I asked him if I could climb up to the observation tower. He asked an officer, who said it was rather strenuous, which it was, but he allowed it. I had observed the Border numerous times from the tower of Point Alpha and now I was suddenly on the other side. My God, am I awake or am I dreaming? Am I really looking now from East to West? As often as I was on Point Alpha with Domestic and Foreign high officials, I never forgot the message, that the history of this place would not let itself be changed, and now this! Happy, fascinated and shaken, all of these feelings at the same time, I experienced a bath of indescribable emotions.

How could you evaluate all of this in distance of the years? The peaceful demonstrations of the GDR citizens in autumn of 1989 completed that which was begun on the 17 June 1953. Throughout all these long years, the call for democracy, freedom and human dignity had never quite died. The people in the GDR had to take a long and sacrificial way, but they succeeded. Therefore, from a historical point of view, the aggression free demonstration is and remains the most important spiritual and moral foundation of the German Reunification. That is the point, the heart of what we celebrate on each 3 October. The peaceful uprising of the people was in the end the triggering impulse for the collapse of the entire east block. The citizens of the GDR wrote an unequalled historical success story because: their courageous demonstration peacefully ended the competition between two irreconcilable ideologies; they succeeded in transforming the block communistic state-directed economy within a short time into a free, even if not social market economy everywhere; and because with this, the foundation for a united Europe in peace and freedom was laid. Thus this revolution became the event which turned Germany once again into a cultural nation in the heart of Europe, and qualified it to live up to its responsibility in the world – also in the role of mediator between America, Asia, and Europe as well as partner for Africa, South America and all the developing countries.
The determination and the guarantee of security from the West Allies, together with the German's drive for freedom prepared the way for the "Wende", but the battalions, the tanks and the rockets did not culminate it; it was the people of the GDR! This process was supported by a few politicians, who in that moment when the seam of this story touched them, grabbed it courageously and determinedly – a fantastic

deed. The people of Thuringia, Saxony and the other new countries have all good reason, with a strong sense of self confidence, to be proud of what they have accomplished. On this eventful day in the year 2005, as George Bush sr., Michail Gorbatschow and Helmut Kohl came to Point Alpha, this was impressively confirmed by these crown witnesses of history. I would like to make public what the previous American president said to me at this opportunity at the end of our talks, which was more than just small talk. Impressed by what he had just experienced, George Bush said: "If I had known then, what I know now, I would have definitely changed my appointments in order to stay longer. Point Alpha is an impressive place of history for Germans and Americans." A huge compliment!

2. The Accomplished, the Current Situation, a Perspective

We now have freedom of press and travel, as well as participation in all democratic and communal autonomy. Thus, all of the conditions, which the citizens of previous GDR need to be able to independently structure and manage their own lives, exist. Whoever had the advantage, as I did, of growing up in West German, has a hard time of it imagining what it means to not be able to run his own life, what it means to be told what to do and to live in the constant fear that even the smallest little corner of private life could still be minimized or even totally removed. But I do not find it at all difficult to feel the happiness for all those who have won a new standard of life. Prime Minister Dieter Althaus once said in Erfurt that he is happy and thankful that no one can force a political ethos from his daughter if she wanted to start job training or advance in her career. That is exactly the point: Humans are destined for freedom and especially for structuring their own lives. I share the happiness of the Thuringian Prime Minister!

The Solidarity Pact 1 exists since 1990 for which 250 Billion Euro were raised. And the

Solidarity Pact II with another 156 Billion followed. I would like to write in the register for all the Bundestag Members: don't start changing this, because this help is still needed in the new countries of East Germany! The final amount of investment for the development of the East is actually even larger because the investment special funds and the entire enormous amount for the social services still have to be calculated. According to the calculations of experts, it is another 1.2 Trillion Euros! Which country in the world has ever achieved such a show of strength! Germany and the Germans can be proud of these fantastic achievements which are evident everywhere. Sometimes I hear comments in my city that the streets in Thuringia are even better than in Hesse – sometimes they are! But this can only be a good reason for honest pleasure for us "Wessies".

The same applies to the modern communication system or for the infra-structure per se, and for the maintenance of the old cultural city – often in the last minute. It was exactly these cities which interested and fascinated me, where I gathered not only interesting communal political impressions, but also experienced happy and thankful encounters with absolutely wonderful people who proved that no one and nothing can suppress citizen pride for ever. In a few individual cases, I experienced situations where I had to speak a word of warning; for example in Görlitz. This was where, in the GDR era, the demolition of the unique ensemble of the city center was planned. In its place, the infamous block building. The "Wende" came about just in time to prevent this disgrace on the cultural city and to save the Görlitz inner city as an important city protected monument. But what happened afterwards? The Görlitz citizens were suddenly sick of the ribbed glasses in the windows of their houses. This attack on the historical construction elements could be deterred only through an incredible effort. In order to maintain culture, having a sense of culture is necessary. Since this was only ideologically defined in the GDR era, it had to now first be developed. This is, to a great extent, accomplished and so it was proven

once again here and in other issues what a great gift the reunification was in every sense of the word, regardless if we are at home in the East or the West.

Since the "Wende", 500,000 new businesses have been opened. This proves that the total reorganization of the economy was necessary and it shows at the same time the enormous creativity and industriousness of the people living there. **The investment, in the classical sense, was the essential condition for the development of the East, but the human investment – people – was the key to success.**

What is the situation today? Are we a people? To quote Thomas Aquinas, "He who does not burn, cannot ignite others". We must all have the unbreakable will to become a people again. We cannot create the same standards of living all at once everywhere, but comparative living conditions must be established and the development process towards complete equality must be supported as best as possible. But not the government is meant; rather each and everyone one of us. Why has the happiness over the great event in autumn of 1989 left us so quickly? What an elation on that November day and how fast disillusion set in. We have to think about it. What could we, each of us, do to make things better? No, it really is not true that only the government of the Federation and the parliament, ministers, individual members of some commissions are responsible; all of us are responsible. Each of us can do something so that unity also takes place in the minds and that finally everyone understands what a great gift the Unity is. It must be a collective concern, to accept this gift thankfully and to make the best of it. Only when we achieve this, have we built the foundation of the German Unity on solid ground. I will give ten reasons why the elation of the first hours vanished so quickly:
great events fade the further in the past they lay. A teenager today more likely knows the name of the goal keeper of Bayern Munich than he could explain what happened in 1953, 1961, and 1989 in Germany. This recognition pulls the topic of "school" into

view. We need to ask the critical question – how much is actually being done to deal comprehensively with the topics of People's Uprising, Building of the Wall and Reunification. If things are not to be forgotten, then history and values must be transferred in the education at home and in the school.

The knowingly passing on of false information and/or the misinterpretation, based on incomplete records, of the costs of the Reunification has had their effects: the politicians and the media are in demand here.

The lacking awareness in many of the uniqueness of the democratic achievement has impeded the correct estimation of the political, the mental, cultural and the economic standing of the "Wende" on a national and international level.

The preconceptions and the jealousy debates of old cadre, new ignoramus, or the eternal "yesterday people" encumber the collective way to the future because not all of them have the capabilities needed to establish their individual opinions on all issues.

The lack of reflective and critical handling of the past has transformed the facts of the insufferable conditions (which were so often described as unacceptable) and created a totally redundant wave of nostalgia.

The lack of general social consensus on the necessary reforms has blocked the sense of responsibility for the future.

The "you owe me" mentality which the citizens of the new countries have all too gladly taken over from the old German Republic and incorporated in their accustomed "provide for me" mentality, has suppressed the memory of the long time prevailing shortages which existed then in the GDR.

The unspeakably stupid comparison between winners and losers in the Unity are no longer populist slogans.

The ever existent paternalism of the East and the so difficult to change subvention mentality of the West mutually create a tangled situation through which lasting future concepts can only overcome with the greatest of difficulty. A few politically and psychologically displaced statements which can be heard or read in election campaigns have come close to doubting our political competency.

What comes of this? It is high time to wake up, rethink and thoroughly convince ourselves of the accomplishments and what they mean for all the people of Europe. What a person is made of comes through culture, spirit of freedom and human dignity. But this takes character, education and the right basis. In many minds, the non-culture of "sentimentalism" has planted itself. The only possible answer to it is, away from all the horrible complainers, away from the pessimists, and off to the optimistic base idea. We can do it, we have managed to accomplish unbelievable up to now and we will also master all that still has to be done. We must apply our great conviction, our belief in ourselves and determined action against the laming poison of these permanent complaints. The main question is not what the German Unity cost us but rather what in the world could have been more worth the cost of the German Unity? This is the question which needs to be posed and always answered with the comment that the German Unity did not only end the Cold War but also made it possible that a matchless peace union could develop in Europe. Therefore the investments we made in the German Reunification were investments in peace and freedom in entire Europe! ! **After all of the terror and suffering the 20th Century brought us, a better investment in the future can not be found.**

If we asked the question what the defense preparation and undertakings in the Cold War had cost, and if we had a cost-benefit calculation for these undertakings in comparison to the cost of development in the East, it would be clear to at least the generous critics where the civil profit lays. All of us who lived in the Federal Republic of Germany (FRG) needed to repeatedly call to mind that all Germans, regardless whether they were at home in the GDR or the FRG, are mutually and equally responsible for the crimes of the national socialists and the victims of WWII, whereby the people of the GDR had to pay a much higher price. If this is correct, then it is also correct and above all fair, that now Thuringia, Saxony and all of the new countries should receive the larger part of the profit and finally the chances which the Federal Republic have had from the beginning. Even more so because, as we should honestly admit, even without the cost of the German Unity, the Federal Republic would have had economical, social and trade problems at the end of the 20th century because in some respects we had lived too good and too long beyond our means. That is another reason why the reorganizing of the West is the most important basis for the development of the East. In face of our responsibility to the Creation and our children, we must certainly make a few changes, but definitely not in the support of the people in the new countries of East Germany. Here we do have a debt. **It is time to rationally understand what we emotionally so elatedly celebrated in the beginning.**

3. What Should the Consequences Be?

This could mean motivating the people in the new countries to stay, and encouraging them to apply their sense of pride and contribute a bit of pioneer work in the East. It might also mean encouraging those who once left the GDR and made it to a position of success and wealth in the Federal Republic, to perform an act of solidarity to the homeland and go back, or at least to support it in a special way. Werner Deschauer, from Geisa, who became a successful business man in Bochum, is a great example of this. If only there were more Deschauers, or people like him, who by means of their behavior – support is not always in terms of money – would show that they have not forgotten their origins.

In due respect to the facts, it is also necessary occasionally to tell the people of the new countries that it is not their individual lives in the GDR that are being discussed, but rather it is about processing the terrible legacy of a communistic regime. The West Germans are challenged to be sensitive, understanding and generous in their approach because we are not the appointed judges or the wise moral apostles who are meant to preach or judge from a higher position. More to the point, we must instigate the dialogues and create a "we feeling". We the Thuringians, we the Hessians, and we the Germans in Thuringia and Hessia in the God-given unified Germany. The point at which subjective reaction and objective results touch, is always where the feelings of the people are the topic. To know this is important because it keeps you from becoming arrogant. Whenever an East German feels inferior, the West German has, in case of doubt, failed. The self named consultants and far too many so called experts who swarmed into the GDR after the "Wende", with their extreme amount of self-interest and often a glaring lack of sensitivity, have caused damage, not only to the hearts and minds of the people who trusted them but also to the cause itself.

If we want to take all of this to heart, then we must be unconditionally willing to learn from one another and we must encourage each other to master the future together. In the west, the foolhardy ranting of the political greenness of the frustrated East German permanent problem child must fall silent. And in the East the longing for the "good old days", which never existed, must come to an end. It is absurd, yes, counterproductive, when film producers and book authors melancholically talk about how wonderful the GDR could have been if the GDR had not had the SED, Stasi, Bautzen, mines and barbed wire. Where is the sense in this? No, we must look forward. We must hold on to what the future is. **All political parties are requested to finally work out a clever and humanitarian strategy of convincing the people in the new countries instead of simply serving them the West German tradionalised recipe. This is the only way we can help them find their national identity in the now larger Germany and help to participate in the organizing of a new eco-social free market economy. I mention this deliberately because it does not help anyone to denounce the serious mistakes of socialism without confronting the weakness of capitalism at the same time. It is time to think about what needs to be de-**

veloped further in the established system. Marion Gräfin Dönhoff, an amazing woman in a number of ways with whom I feel a very strong affinity, wrote a book years ago, titled "Humanize Capitalism" a book which is still, even more so now in face of the total globalization, a remarkably relevant book; a book which puts its finger directly on the sore spot. We need capitalism and the entrepreneurial success=profit, because only the investments and jobs guarantee and secure the social system. But we should not practice inhumane capitalism in which the shareholder value mentality becomes the only deciding factor. Something has gone wrong when so many people in the GDR, who put all their hopes into the free and social market economy which was so successful for us after WWII, only experience it as a cold mechanism. This has to hurt us because it proves that we were not able to convince in the fundamentals and to make practical success possible. It is of even greater importance today to take away the fear, to encourage and to tell stories of hope, which thank God, do exist. A step in the right direction would be if young people came regularly to Point Alpha to find out for themselves what happened then, to discover what has happened in the meantime and then to report where special success has been achieved in co-operation between the East and the West. Again I refer to the good example of Werner Deschauer and his wife.

With this kind of positive change, a constitutional patriotism could develop. This term, which molded Rolf Sternberger of the Heidelberg School for Political Science, is in combination with both terms – constitution and patriotism – completely harmless. It is about the citizen's compassionate and participatory friendship in their constitutional state, our reunified Germany. If this ever happened, it would make things in Germany a lot better because constitutional patriotism is based on pride and self confidence which are immune to querulousness. Just as the Americans, when they sing their national hymn, laying their hands over their hearts, as demonstration of their patriotic spirit, we, also for the same reasons, should demonstrate through our behavior that we are proud of Germany. The worst thinkable example to this point is often the athletes of a national team when they nearly impassively line up and do not even open their mouths when the national hymn is sung.

Point Alpha is and remains the unparalleled Warning, Memorial and Meeting place where it is easy to recognize what we were spared. I can only hope that I, retrospectively thinking and foresightedly reminding, have outlined the story of the German Unity and thereby have encouraged, each day anew in the hope of exchanging interest and partnerships, the active quest for encounters beyond all borders, above all, those in our minds.

This must grow and ripe und it needs time. Let us be patient with others and with ourselves. We will be more successful in this, the sooner we understand that "love your neighbor" is an old Christian daily virtue which demands credible thinking and action, aims at sustainability and is conserved by respect of the differences. The old GDR era, which once, irony of fate, was called the new time, has to give way to the true new time of spirit, cultural and honest solidarity and social behavior of a united Germany. This begins in the minds and must become a matter of heart. Therefore, we need consciousness of reality, more mutual trust, clear goals, patience, the belief in ourselves and our country, and surely a great deal of money for a number of years. But each one of us must know: **One can only use the role model he has, to be a role model for others. Only those who have stabile values are in the position of conveying their values credibly. No task is larger, no goal more worthy!**

To sum up: The call "We are a people" has thank God not faded, but we are not yet really this people; the process is not complete. Point Alpha is a place where these developments can receive the right impulse, because the danger of a third world war is realistically comprehensible here. That is also why, at Point Alpha – easier felt here than anywhere else – there is such a great feeling of happiness over being protected through the good nature of fate from something terrible. I feel this each time anew **and with gratefulness I think of the American Regiment, the 14th and the 11th ACR, who did their duty so long on the border of freedom until they could say with pride and satisfaction: well done!**

We are not yet that people that we were, but one day we will be. But, even if this remains our largest task for the next time, we still have all good reason to be thankful for what we have achieved. With Gods blessing, we will succeed in the last steps as well.

Picture credits

image selection: Verein Grenzmuseum Rhön. Point Alpha e.V.

Michael Reichel (ari): cover picture

Archives Point Alpha: S. 6, 7 (above), 8, 10, 11, 12, 13, 14, 15, 16, 17 (above), 21 (left above), 27, 32, 33, 34, 38, 39 (oben), 43, 48 (at the bottom left hand corner and right), 50, 53

Volker Feuerstein: S. 17 (down), 24, 36, 37, 40, 46, 47, 48 (links oben)

Archives Family Bednarek: S. 7 (center)

Artus Atelier: S. 9 (above), 26 (left above)

Gerhard Daniel: S. 9 (down), 18

Private Archives Stoll: S.7 (down)

Walter Sandner: S. 20 (above)

Archives BGS Hünfeld: S. 20 (down), 22, 23

Archives BGS Fulda: S. 25

Archives BGS: S. 21 (right, center, down), 28

Steven Steininger: S. 26 (on the top right, down), 35, 39 (down)

Peter Blume: S. 29 (down), 30, 31 (above)

Eduardo E. Barretto: S. 29 (above)

Jim Payne: S. 31 (at the bottom left hand corner, down right)

Winfried Möller: S. 41, 57 (left above), 62, 63

Foto Express Gebr. Salzmann GbR: S. 42, 44, 54, 55, 56, 65, 66, 68

Archives Office for Federal Fortune: S. 49

Rudolf Peter Karpe: S. 51

Archives Police Gotha: S. 58

Carsten Kallenbach: S. 59, 60 (down), 61

Daniel Dittmar: S. 60 (above)

Karl-Heinz Burckhardt: S. 64

It was not always possible, to clearly determine the owners of illustration rights. Entitled rights will naturally be compensated for within the framework of usual agreements.